NANA PRAH
Love and Handicrafts

ARTISTS OF GHANA SERIES

First Published in Great Britain in 2023 by
LOVE AFRICA PRESS
103 Reaver House, 12 East Street, Epsom KT17 1HX
www.loveafricapress.com

Text copyright © Nana Prah, 2023

All rights reserved.
No part of this publication may be reproduced, stored or transmitted in any form by any means, electronic, mechanical, photocopying or otherwise, without the prior permission of the publisher, except in the case of brief quotations embodied in reviews.

The right of Nana Prah to be identified as author of this work has been asserted by them in accordance with the Copyright, Design and Patents Act, 1988

This is a work of fiction. Names, places, events and incidents are either the products of the author's imagination or used fictitiously. Any resemblance to actual persons, living or dead, is purely coincidental.

Available as eBook and paperback

ARTISTS OF GHANA SERIES

Love and Hiplife
Love and Handicrafts

NANA PRAH
Love and Handicrafts
ARTISTS OF GHANA SERIES

Chapter One

Back straight and chin up, Precious Kpodo tugged down the back of her royal blue scrub top as she closed her car door. The butterflies fluttering in her stomach would go away as soon as she'd explained her presence to the family expecting her colleague Daniel for the initial at home physiotherapy session. Just yesterday, Daniel had decided to take a more lucrative position without informing the Aboagye family of the change.

He'd claimed to be in a rush travelling to his latest job, so it had been useless trying to convince him to inform the family himself that he wouldn't be able to work with them. A formal introduction of her as Mr Aboagye's new home physiotherapist would have given them a choice in the matter rather than having someone being thrust on them.

Precious always prided herself on her professionalism, and Daniel's greedy, selfish act made her appear like less of one. The family hadn't even gotten the chance to approve of her as a second choice. Her skills as a physiotherapist were on par with Daniel's—some would argue better—but maybe if she attempted to be charming, stepping on others to get what she wanted like he did, she'd get more private clients outside of her job in the hospital. Despite how fun and beneficial it might be, her direct and honest nature would leave her feeling forever remorseful if she manipulated people the way he did. Either she did what had to be done the right way, or she wouldn't profit at all.

Daniel had given her the client's number last night when he'd asked her for the massive favour. She'd opened her mouth to reject the offer once he'd mentioned that he hadn't told them about the change of plans, but Mr Aboagye needed a physiotherapist, and she was available. She'd worked with him for three sessions while he'd been admitted in the hospital, so he knew her. The opportunity was too good to pass up, so she'd agreed. If he didn't want her as his home therapist, then she'd recommend someone else.

However, there'd been no answer or return call when she'd tried many times to contact the client. Considering that Mr Aboagye had been discharged from the hospital yesterday, they'd probably been busy settling him into his home. If Daniel had been responsible and taken care of contacting them in the first place, she wouldn't be surprising Mr Aboagye at six a.m. to do a job they'd hired a different person for. What could go wrong?

With one large inhale of the cool, dry, foggy Harmattan air which slightly irritated her throat but helped to soothe the frustration she still held against her colleague, she pressed the doorbell. Only a few seconds passed before the small gate was opened by a man whose dark eyes scanned her from head to toe. She hadn't missed the interest that had flashed in his gaze during his assessment. By the time his eyes reached hers again, that spark was gone, his expression now stern. Bordering on irritated.

Her attention to detail served her well as she assessed the nearly six-foot-tall man. Rich dark-brown skin, high cheekbones, and a slim-bridged nose with a wide base, ending above a moustache connected to a goatee that emphasized two-toned dusky pink and brown lips.

Just the kind of direct handsomeness that appealed to her. His broad shoulders were covered by a lavender dress shirt moulded against flat abs, tucked into grey trousers emphasising his muscular thighs. She brought her vision back to his face, and heat swirled in her stomach as their gazes held.

He shifted half a step forward and then seemed to think better of it when he shook his head and cleared his throat. "How may I help you?"

The briskness of his deep voice snagged her out of the unexpected attraction that had wound them together, reminding her of her mission. Ready to get through the hard part of the encounter, she brought her professionalism to the forefront and lifted her lips into a smile that combined friendliness and confidence. Might as well state what she wanted to happen. The explanations would come soon enough.

"Good morning. My name is Precious Kpodo." She held up her hospital name badge. "I'm Emmanuel Aboagye's physiotherapist."

His head cocked to the right and then the left, reminding her of an owl, giving her the impression he was an analytical man as the seconds extended between them.

"No, you aren't," he said with an enunciation of every word as if he found her to be dim-witted. "We made an arrangement with Daniel Boakye."

Daniel had put her in this awkward position, and although her confidence wavered for a moment, she refused to look away from this man's intense stare. She wouldn't be intimidated, especially when her intention was to help Mr Aboagye regain his strength and mobility no matter how she came to be there.

"I'm sorry to be the one to inform you, but Daniel couldn't make it. He had to travel at the last minute." Holding up her phone, she waved it. "I've attempted several times to call the number he gave me, but I haven't been able to get through."

"Show me," he ordered as he reached out a hand.

She clenched her jaw to keep it from dropping in shock. His rudeness made her seem more like someone out to con him personally rather than a healthcare worker, in uniform, with a badge, at a time her colleague would've been there if he could've been.

Remembering this wasn't his fault and that she was a professional, she ignored his abrupt behaviour and input her numerical password, bringing up the recent calls before handing him the phone.

He scrolled up the list of twenty failed attempts with his thumb. "This is my mother's number. She never knows where her phone is."

Precious chuckled. Her mother was the same way. At his sharp glance, she removed the mirth from her countenance and took her device back.

"I think mine hides her phone intentionally," she admitted to build rapport. "Now that you have the proof that I tried to get in contact, can I please come in and see Mr Aboagye now?"

Still blocking her entry, he crossed his arms over his chest. "We hired Daniel. That's who we want."

Now he was being single-minded, and that wouldn't help anyone. If Daniel was the only one he'd work with, then the client wouldn't get therapy for at least a month while Daniel toiled on a more lucrative assignment.

Rather than let her annoyance get the better of her, she dug deep for patience, then nodded in a conciliatory manner.

"I understand the change of physiotherapists may be disconcerting when you were expecting Daniel," she stated in the calm yet stern tone she used when her clients got frustrated with their inability to perform an exercise immediately. "I work with him at 37 Hospital, and he asked me to fill in for him. I apologize that he wasn't able to inform you of this himself, but he had to travel to Bolgatanga by special request."

Greedy man that he is. Everyone wanted more money, but she wouldn't shirk off her responsibilities to obtain it. She reached into her bag and pulled out her CV. Having to prove herself with almost every client, both in and out of the hospital, grated on her nerves, but she was a stranger to this man. All thanks to Daniel.

He flicked his gaze to the papers she held without making an attempt to take them.

Precious took a deep breath. "I worked with Mr Aboagye a few times while he was in the hospital. I'm sure he remembers me. We got along well. If you'd let me in, he could decide for himself if he wants to work with me or not."

Still no reaction from the man whose stiff confrontational stature reminded her of the soldiers she frequently came in contact with at the hospital. Why hadn't any of Mr Aboagye's family members that she'd met answered the gate? That would've made things so much easier.

Since he wouldn't read it for himself, she proceeded to verbalize her CV. "I graduated first class from KNUST as a physiotherapist. I'm in good standing with the Ghana Physiotherapy Association. I have worked in the physiotherapy department at 37 Military Hospital for the past twelve years, since graduation, but took time off to get my MSc in Physiotherapy from the University of Nottingham on the neuromuscular pathway."

His brows raised a fraction. "And you returned to Ghana voluntarily?"

Out of everything she'd said, *that's* what had piqued his interest? She held in the sigh that threatened to reveal her increasing frustration. This was about what she could do for Mr Aboagye as a physiotherapist, not her personal decision to not make a life abroad. If he were anyone else, she'd ignore the question and continue with convincing him to let her enter the house so she could start her work. Without knowing his relationship to Mr Aboagye, she understood it was important to be cordial to him. "My family, friends, and career are here. Ghana is home, and I wanted to help my people."

A grunt came from his chest, as if he were calling her ten types of stupid. Or maybe it was pride in her decision? She hoped for the latter.

The paper in her hand ruffled as she shook it. "I have extensive experience in hemiparesis stroke recovery, like your father suffers from. My references are listed here. You can also call Daniel to verify." *Good luck reaching him.*

"Osei, what's taking so long?" The gate opened further, and a smaller, female version of the man appeared.

Precious smiled as she recognized Mr Aboagye's oldest daughter, Serwaa.

The young woman pushed past him with open arms and embraced her. "Precious! What are you doing here?"

Precious squeezed back before releasing Serwaa with a grin that couldn't have been slapped off. Serwaa would prove her claim to the disgruntled man.

"Daniel had to travel so he sent me to work with your father." She shot the man an accusatory glance. "If he's okay with it."

"I'm sure he will be. Come in."

Precious accompanied Serwaa as they walked past the man onto the compound. His clean, fresh, woodsy scent reclaimed her attention, reminding her of her initial attraction before he became annoying.

"You know her?" The baritone voice followed them.

"What gave it away, Osei? She worked with Dada at the hospital. To be honest," Serwaa added in a loud whisper to Precious, "Dada said he enjoyed his time with you more than he did with Daniel. He said something about you making things easier to learn. He was disappointed when Osei hired Daniel."

Pride that her good work had been recognized bubbled up in her chest as Precious arched a brow up at Osei in an I-told-you-so manner.

"I've never met you."

Serwaa shook her head. "My brother thinks he's omnipotent and knows everything and everyone. Never mind that he only met Daniel once when he came to visit during Dada's two-week stay."

"But you're a woman," Osei added.

This man, paa! Disappointed and angry, Precious pivoted to glower. How dare he belittle her and what she'd accomplished with her career? She'd cited him her credentials, and he still saw her as *just* a woman? As analytical as he'd appeared earlier, he'd let ignorance overtake his intelligence.

Anxious to tell him a thing or two about how well a woman could do any job she put her mind to, she diverted her attention towards a palm tree and allowed its swaying leaves to calm her. She'd had to deal with these types of men, and women, particularly in Ghana, throughout her career. The major lesson she'd learned was to always be professional, no matter how much she wanted to take them down a peg. Since the family wanted to be involved in Mr Aboagye's therapy, he'd learn just how powerful she was as a physiotherapist and never use those derogatory words again.

Returning her sharp gaze to him, she'd give him a chance to explain. If he didn't do so to her satisfaction, he'd receive a lesson on feminism and the basics of physiotherapy he'd be quoting to his grandchildren one day.

Chapter Two

Osei Aboagye knew he'd walked into a brick wall of trouble as two pair of dark eyes scowled at him. Defeated by his own outrageous comment, he held up both hands and took a step back. He hadn't meant it the way it had come out, and more importantly, his sister understood. They'd been raised by the same woman who could carry three crates of beverages at one time even at the age of sixty-four. Women and strength went hand in hand in his world.

But for the past two weeks, the stress and fear of dealing with his father's stroke had weighed heavily on him, and it just happened to turn off his common sense right when he'd needed it most.

"I mean, you can't be more than five-foot-six. How are you able to help such a big man? He'll knock you over." His mind hissed at his continued idiocy. What was wrong with him?

Both women braced their hands on their hips, in a wide stance, superhero style.

"Precious is taller than me," Serwaa said. "Are you saying I'm weak?"

"Of course not." He swiped at the sweat rolling down the side of his face. If he tried to explain, he'd just dig himself in deeper. He wanted his father to be able to walk again, to be as fierce as he had been before. He'd been scared out of his mind when he'd gotten the news of the strongest man he knew being incapacitated in the hospital. Most importantly, he wanted his father to live a long life. He'd never been on the cusp of losing someone he loved before, and it was taking a toll he was now paying.

There was only one way out of this. He released his pride as he dropped his arms to his sides. "I'm sorry. Your qualifications were impressive, and since you've worked with my father before and he preferred you over Daniel, you must be more than capable."

Serwaa nodded and walked into the house, understanding that his apology meant he'd claimed complete responsibility and the conversation was over.

Precious however continued to hold him captive with her narrowed eyes that looked like she'd eviscerate him if she wouldn't end up in jail for it. He held his ground, accepting that whatever she'd dish out, he deserved.

"Physiotherapy is not about tossing people around. It's a science where we use techniques and manoeuvres to assist the client to mobilize. The last time I worked with your father, he was stronger in mind and body than when he'd first been admitted. He'd tolerated weight bearing on his affected side for several seconds as we helped him transfer from the bed to the chair." She paused, and her shoulders relaxed. "As you mentioned, I'm capable at my job. I accept your apology."

Relieved that she wouldn't hold a grudge, he cleared his throat. "Thank you. I've taken up enough of your time. My father is looking forward to us learning how to help him get better faster."

Her full cheeks lifted with the grin taking over her glossy lips. He ignored the flip of his stomach at the sight of a genuine smile aimed at him. Her cocoa-brown skin looked radiant despite the grey fogginess of the morning. Large, rounded eyes crinkled slightly at the corners, giving away the possibility that she was older than he'd suspected, or that she tended to smile a lot. For some strange reason, he liked the thought of her being happy.

"I appreciate you wanting to learn the exercises so you can help and encourage your father," she said. "Daniel mentioned that all four of his children jumped at the opportunity to be involved. It will go a long way in Mr Aboagye's recovery."

As the oldest, he bore the responsibility of aiding in his father's recovery. He'd do anything to make it happen. "We want the best for our father, and Daniel said if we learned how to implement the exercises, my father would have a chance of getting stronger faster."

"He's right."

The much-deserved scolding session seemed over because Precious pivoted and went into the house, leaving him to follow. His attention lingered on a behind her scrubs couldn't hide. Her hips didn't curve out from a small waist, but her butt looked firm, yet had a wonderful jiggle to it with every step. An African female with just the right type of thickness.

He'd appreciated her from head to toe when he'd opened the gate. The long eyelashes framing large eyes had lain a shadow on her cheeks when she'd blinked. The fullness of her lips had caught his gaze for longer than it should've when she'd smiled. Beautiful face, intelligence, and she had grit. A magnificent combination.

She's here for my father. Not for me to date.

That hadn't stopped him from taking a deep inhale of her light floral scent as she'd passed by him at the gate. He'd leaned forward to inhale more of it. Perhaps the need to be closer to her had ignited the foolishness he'd uttered. It didn't matter because a woman like Precious was most likely involved with someone, but it also didn't matter because she was off-limits. The name Precious Kpodo made it clear she was Ewe. The people from the Volta Region could be classmates, acquaintances, and colleagues, yet never to be dated. Not in his father's house, particularly if you wanted peace in your life and to be accepted within the family.

He detested his father's tribalistic sentiment, but he'd never crossed the man and gone out with anyone who was Ewe before either. At university, he'd had the freedom and accessibility to date anyone he'd wanted without his father discovering it, but had stayed away from Ewes. He hadn't taken the time to scrutinize himself to discover if it had been by design or intention, but his father's warning had always been at the back of his mind. These days, he had no time for relationships. Twelve-to-fourteen-hour days at his corporate job kept wearing him down.

When not in his office, he unwound by shaping reclaimed wood. Although his hobby didn't bring him enough money to do it as his sole career, creating furniture and home décor made him happier than dealing with the continuous employment and personal issues he intervened in as a human resources assistant manager. A job he'd once enjoyed before it threatened to swallow his whole life.

The concept of forging a relationship with a woman had dropped to the wayside. His career proved too time-consuming to get to know someone sufficiently enough to assess if they were compatible, so he stayed single.

At thirty-five, it wasn't as if he had to marry any time soon, despite the pressure his mother and aunties had started to place on him. He'd witnessed friends and colleagues rush into marriage only for them to crash and burn. Not him. Short encounters of fun and sex were all he could dedicate himself to. Maybe when he one day became a manager, he could relax. Unless he quit the HR world first. It would be a dream come true to sell his crafts on a full-time basis without starving.

Looking at how things were going in Ghana and the forecasted declining market, it would probably never happen. He had to find a way to be okay with that. Better to be miserable and have money in your pocket than to be broke. His step hitched with uncertainty at the thought of continuing to exist with no passion or joy. In the end, survival always trumped happiness, though, and he'd have to accept it.

Osei joined the others in his parents' large bedroom just in time to witness the hugs and greetings between Precious, his three siblings, and his mother. How could he have missed meeting her when he'd been to visit his father almost every day in the hospital?

It might've helped if I'd stayed for longer than twenty minutes during my lunch break and spent quality time with him. Pushing away the guilt, he listened as Precious taught them how to help his father with leg and arm exercises while he lay in bed.

They all took a try at assisting his father with the exercises. Not normally the most patient man, his father not only tolerated the attention, but encouraged it. Osei didn't blame him. Having his independence taken away by a stroke had not only scared but changed him.

The man Osei knew as impatient, driven, and brisk had been forced to slow down.

Take a lesson from him before it's too late.

His mind had been saying that a lot since his father's stroke. Too much. The hard part? He'd wanted to listen. He just didn't know how without giving up everything he'd worked so hard for.

Using the techniques Precious taught them, they took turns helping his father into the chair and then back onto the bed.

"I'm tired," his father admitted in a still slurred, but much clearer voice than he'd had two weeks ago.

"You've done very well, Mr Aboagye," Precious said. "You've gained more strength in your left arm and leg since I last worked with you."

His grin appeared most prominent on the right side of his face, even though his lips didn't droop as much on the left as it had even a week ago. "Thank you. I will improve."

"I'm sure you will. Would you like to rest in here or in the hall?" she asked.

"The hall."

Precious showed the family how to unlock the chair and had his youngest sister, Dorcas, wheel it into the other room.

"I know this is a sensitive topic," Precious said to his father. "I brought the commode you ordered. With your support, one of your family members can help you onto it and then wheel you to the bathroom. It should settle over the toilet."

His mother, who had no issues with discussing anyone's bowel patterns, stepped forward. "Yes, using the commode was convenient at the hospital so we decided to purchase one to give him more independence."

Precious nodded. "It was a great choice."

Embarrassed about the personal topic, Osei didn't want to be anywhere near the conversation. Not when Precious, someone he might've wanted to impress if circumstances weren't stacked against them, was in the middle of it so he slunk back. His three siblings suddenly discovered something amazing on their phone to occupy their attention.

"We'll let you rest now, Mr Aboagye," Precious said. "I'll see you later today."

"Have a good day, Precious," the former secondary school head master said with a wave of his unaffected hand. "Thank you."

They took the cue of his father's eyes drifting closed to leave him to sleep.

Precious turned to Serwaa. "Can you please help me bring the commode in?"

"I'll help you," Osei volunteered.

The straight hair of her ponytail swung to the side when she tipped her head and quirked a brow.

"Not that Serwaa, Dorcas, or Mama can't help you." He circumvented the reflexive comment about the equality of the sexes that he could foresee flying out of her mouth. "But I'm responsible for getting Dada out of bed and ready in the mornings. I'll start with unloading the commode."

He walked towards the door before she could respond. Sensing her tailing him, he held himself back from stopping abruptly so she'd stumble into him. Would her hands sear his skin with her heat as she pressed them against his back to maintain her balance? He could see himself turning and wrapping his arms around her waist and shoulders in an attempt to stabilize her. He silenced a groan as his groin twitched at the thought of having Precious pressed flush against him. Knowing the risks, he increased his stride.

When they were out in the compound, she broke the silence. "Will you be the one assisting your father every morning?"

"Yes. I work long hours and won't be able to help much during the day, so I volunteered to assist him in the mornings and to use the toilet if and when he needed it whenever I'm home." It was the absolute least he could do, which made him feel like a bad son for not being able to make more time for the man who had raised him.

He pushed the latch to the small gate over and opened it. When she passed by, the same light, fresh scent he'd smelled earlier embraced him. He took a deep sniff. The tanginess of citrus, sweetness of something floral, and the familiarity of cocoa butter. The cocoa butter might be what kept her skin glowing and enticing. Shaking his head to clear it, he followed her out to the Kia Sportage she'd parked in front of the house.

"It's not heavy, just cumbersome," Precious said as she unlocked and lifted the hatch of her vehicle where the back seat had been folded over to make room for the commode.

Rather than jump right in and pull the equipment out, he waited for her to instruct him. He hadn't gotten as far as he had in life by not learning lessons. The first of the day had been to never presume anything about Precious Kpodo and her capabilities. Her teaching session had been impressive. She'd been right about his father being able to do most of the work while they supported. He tamped down the need to apologize again for his earlier condescending behaviour towards her. Since she'd already forgiven him, he'd do the same for himself.

"If you grab that end, I'll get this one."

They got the commode out of the vehicle and headed back to his house.

"I noticed you ignored your phone despite it buzzing during the session." Precious grinned over at him.

He returned the smile with ease despite his desire to check the messages that had come through. "My mother threatened to take a hammer to it if I didn't pay attention. Since you'll be with us for a while, you need to know that whatever she says she's going to do, she will. She's not one to joke."

"I noticed. While your father is the funny one. An opposites attract kind of thing?"

"Only in that regard. They're more like birds of the same feather when it comes to everything else. Particularly how driven they are. That's why I can see him back on his feet and walking on his own." After the session with Precious, he no longer had doubts about it happening, which left him both relieved and grateful.

"I agree. And with such a supportive family, hopefully, he'll get there."

Everyone in the house had found their own places to be so the pathway to his parent's master bedroom lay clear. They settled the commode outside the door of the bathhouse. Precious unlocked the wheels and pushed it in and over the toilet.

"Perfect." She glanced around the large space. "The bath area has a ledge. It would've been convenient if it was level."

"A mason is coming by to do that on Wednesday."

"That's wonderful. It makes a difference to have a full bath which he can do sitting on the commode. Do you need any advice on how to give someone one?"

You could demonstrate on me, if you want. A vision of them naked and soapy flashed into his mind, and he looked away from her, afraid she could see the deliciously naughty thoughts his mind had conjured.

"I'll let you know if I do. I have to get to work. I'll see you out." *That was smooth.*

"Okay."

They went to the kitchen and said goodbye to his mother.

"Both of you, come and eat with us," his mother invited. "I made yam, *kobi*, and eggs."

Precious grimaced at the amount of sodium the salted tilapia contained. "I don't think he should be eating kobi."

"Don't worry, I learned from the nutritionist about what my husband should eat. I soaked the fish, removing most of the salt first so it's fine. Emmanuel won't find it as tasty, but at least, it won't raise his blood pressure."

"Thanks, Mama," Osei said. "But I'll be late if I don't leave right now."

His mother clicked her teeth. "You work in human resources, why do they stress you so much?" She waved towards Precious. "It's not as if you're in healthcare saving lives."

She hadn't dropped a bombshell about the pressures of his job in a while. The harassment she gave him about working too much was justified, if not exasperating. As an entrepreneur, his mother repeatedly emphasised the benefits of him working for himself rather than investing his energy into a company that would drop him without a backwards glance. Since there was nothing he was willing to do to rectify the situation just then, he wouldn't fall into a discussion about it in front of an outsider.

"Have a good day, Mama. I'll see you tonight."

"I need to get going, too, Mrs Aboagye. I'll be back this afternoon at four-thirty."

"Please call me Aunty Theo. Mrs Aboagye is too formal for the miracle you will help perform here with my husband. Both of you have a good day," his mother said as she continued frying the egg-covered yam.

After picking up his tie, bag, and keys from the hall, he escorted Precious to the driver's side of the car and watched her get in. "I know we started off on the wrong foot, but I'm sure things will be better tomorrow."

"As long as you stay away from the sexist comments, we'll be okay."

Her directness hit home, and he held back a wince at how he'd behaved, glad she wasn't vengeful enough to hold it against him. "Will do. I was just shocked. You have converted me into a true believer."

"Good." That glowing smile appeared again. "Is your car parked inside?"

"It's in the shop, so I arranged an Uber." He looked at the app where the vehicle was now thirty minutes away instead of the ten it had initially been a minute ago. He'd thought of walking. Thirty-five minutes wasn't long. He didn't get as much exercise as he needed, and after his father's stroke, he was determined to live his life in a healthier manner. Due to Precious's tutorial, he was running later than he'd expected. His boss wouldn't be kind about him missing their meeting.

Precious' luscious mouth rounded. "Oh. Would you like a ride?"

"I work in North Ridge. You'll get stuck in traffic."

She shrugged. "This is Accra. No matter where I go at this time, I'm trapped. North Ridge isn't far from 37. Cancel the Uber, and I'll give you a ride."

Common sense told him to decline, but his feet took him to the other side of her car and got in. He could pick her brain about her plans for his father's recovery.

Who was he kidding? He wanted to get to know her. Discover why he was so drawn to her while he had the chance. It wasn't as if he'd do anything about it. He may never get the opportunity to be alone with this intriguing woman again, so he may as well take advantage of it while getting to work on time.

Chapter Three

Playing chauffer to the man who had not only been rude to her, but had insulted her as a professional on top of that was not how she'd seen the day progressing. The habit of not minding her own business always ended up more trouble than it was worth. What had made her ask about his car? It didn't matter. If she'd kept her mouth shut and driven off with a hurried goodbye, she wouldn't be feeling as if his presence were pressing into her. Which was silly, considering a console sat between them.

And still, Precious couldn't deny the persistent chemistry making her heart beat a little faster. His concentration was directed towards his phone, but she wanted his eyes on her, conversing as she tried to discover more about why he'd snatched her attention so severely after two hours of meeting him. His mother had mentioned his life was his work. Not the kind of man she'd want to get involved with, even if she allowed herself to.

She snuck a glance over at him as they drove through Cantonments, passing by large, well-maintained houses of people with lifestyles that superseded hers. Why did he have to be such *a fine boy*, as her good friend Toyin would put it. Even the oval shape of his head was impressive. And his hair looked like it had just been cut that morning. Fresh edges? Definitely a turn on. She gripped the steering wheel to keep from smoothing her fingers over his face.

After what she'd experienced that morning, she understood that he brooked no nonsense. She got the impression small talk would irritate him, so she'd kept silent, trying to get her visual fill of him without seeming too obvious about it. Taking in as much as she could of his scent put her on the cusp of becoming lightheaded, her nose wide open for the notes of a cologne that reminded her of a stream rolling through a forest on a warm day. Soothing. Expensive. The kind of scent she'd spray on herself in a shop and pretend she'd been hugged by someone who thought nothing of purchasing lavish things.

Once. She'd only done it at the loneliest time in her life when she'd been studying in the UK. She'd never wanted to feel that alone again, so she'd decided that no matter what opportunity came her way while she was there, she'd return home. She had friends, family, and more than enough dates to keep her satisfied, yet with every sniff, she considered going to the perfume shop and smelling every cologne until she'd hunted his down. Only this time, her fantasy man would have a face. Strong arms. Wide chest. Long muscular thighs that knew how to fill out a pair of trousers in all the right ways.

She shook the inappropriate thought out of her head and lowered her window. He was the son of her client—professionalism was warranted. *He's not your client, though.* It didn't matter—no need to think of him of anything but Emmanuel Aboagye's son. She'd get him to work, and if they ever met up again, she'd have gotten over this little crush.

His fingers tapped against the screen of his phone. Probably an attempt to catch up with the messages that had vibrated in his pocket earlier. From work? Or from his girlfriend? Boyfriend, maybe? Who knew these days? As per the deal with herself, despite the desire to learn more, it was none of her business. Where she was dropping him off was.

"Where do you work?"

"Allegiant Bank," he said in a distracted tone without glancing up from his phone.

The rejection for the business loan his bank had dealt her last month came to mind, and her mood sank a little. She'd been optimistic of the financial assistance they'd give to propel her towards her long-time goal of opening her own physiotherapy centre. Even though she'd presented a spectacular business proposal, she'd been sadly mistaken, and it still hurt. Fourth time was not the charm, after all.

Nerves got the better of her as the car came to a halt in the bumper-to-bumper traffic, and she filled the silence. "Your mother mentioned you were in human resources. Do you enjoy your job?"

Seconds ticked by without a response. Had he heard her? Maybe it was a sign she should shut up. Darn her for not getting her stereo fixed. She took her phone from the cup holder and scanned it for some hiplife music to raise her spirits.

He lifted his head, and his eyes seemed to be pleading before he spoke, his voice slightly lower, pitched with urgency. "If it's okay, I'll answer all the questions you have after I finish this e-mail."

Relieved he wasn't ignoring her because he didn't want to converse, she took pity on him. "That's fine. I was just filling the emptiness. I'll play some music. Do what you need to do."

If she weren't driving, she'd be on her phone, too. Although the law required it, she'd made it a rule not to use her cell while on the road. One accident, although minor, had been more than enough.

She chose her favourite song by Blaise as she looked straight ahead to keep from staring at his profile. Such a strong jawline, and those high cheekbones were stunning.

Stop thinking about him. How could she when he was right there?

Osei slapped his cell down onto his lap. "I enjoy many aspects of my job as an assistant human resource manager."

He'd remembered the question after five minutes of being mentally engaged? Impressive.

"I've been working my way through the ranks for the past ten years, and now, I'm doing mine and my boss' jobs without the added pay."

He hadn't tried to hide the bitterness in his voice. Overworked and underappreciated, she couldn't imagine he was happy where he was. "That sounds stressful."

He nodded. "It is. I like assisting the employees find solutions to their issues."

Precious grimaced as she recalled stories about being called to HR. "What about firing people?"

He shrugged. "Sometimes, it needs to be done. It's part of the job."

That couldn't be a likeable aspect of his work. Just thinking about hurting someone by taking away their income stressed her out. The cars eased forward, and she flowed with the traffic, before stopping again.

"You're gorgeous," his deep voice said in her direction.

Her attention jerked towards him as she blinked several times as if that would clear her ears. The back of her neck tingled, hoping she'd heard correctly and he found her as attractive as she did him. At least then, it wouldn't be one-sided.

Her breath hitched as their gazes locked. "Pardon me?"

He shook his head as if recovering from a trance. "I'm sorry. That was inappropriate."

Osei wasn't a stranger cat-calling her on the streets. He'd given her an unexpected, genuine compliment. This was the second time he'd apologized since they'd met. Despite his arrogance, his pride didn't rule him, and she respected that. Her heart did a little flutter.

Gathering her wits, she smirked. "Are you only now noticing?"

The chuckle erased the tightness in his face. "I definitely noticed. It's just strange that I said it out loud."

That made him sound like he wasn't a ladies' man. Could she believe him? And did it matter? They weren't going anywhere with this strange flirtation. "As long as you keep your insults as inside thoughts, we'll be fine."

"I doubt I'll have any, but will do." He angled his shoulders towards her. "What made you become a physiotherapist?"

Whether he recognized it or not, the question revealed a distinct interest in her and not just her physical attributes. It pleased her more than the compliment. "When I was fifteen, my mother got into a bad car accident as a passenger in a *trotro*. She broke her hip."

The driver of a local mode of public transportation via a small van had been speeding and crashed head-on into another *trotro*. So many people in both vehicles had died, but her foster mother had been lucky to survive.

She sat up straight and gripped the steering wheel to ward off the memory of the terror she'd felt when she'd learned about the accident.

"They operated, and physiotherapy aided her to walk. I was at every session, helping as much as I could as I watched my mother get better. The therapist was kind and patient, both to her and me when I asked my questions. That's when I knew I wanted to do the same job one day. To give hope and mobility to as many as I could help." She sounded like some kind of commercial, but meant every word with all of her heart.

"How's your mother now?"

Her smile came on full force as she spoke. "For years after physio, she walked as if she'd never had the accident. She's had another hip replacement since then. And now, age is catching up with her, slowing her down, but not enough to make her stop working way too hard."

"I didn't realize how old my father had gotten until his stroke. It's made me look at him differently." He tapped a finger against his knee. "Both of my parents. They're only in their sixties and are vibrant, but they won't be around forever. It's a hard blow."

Having recognized the same about her mother, she understood just how he felt and was driven to offer compassion. She rested a hand against his shoulder. The electrical sparks shocked her enough to withdraw and clench her fingers into a fist before placing it on the gear shifter.

Osei's eyes going wide told her he'd felt the same physical reaction.

Not ready to deal with it, she stuck to neutral territory. "It looks like you have a good relationship with your family."

"We're close. What about you?"

Telling her story would put a gloom on the conversation. He'd look at her with pity, and she'd end up in a miserable mood for the rest of the day as the memories of who she'd lost plagued her. She went with her go-to answer when the topic of family came up.

"My mother and I are close." Personal time was over. She craned her neck out the window to look past the vehicles ahead of them. "The cars are moving. There's a police officer directing traffic. Finally!"

"They know there's always a blockage at this junction. It would make sense to have someone present at the same time every day."

Politics, corruption, traffic, police, and the state of the Ghana Blackstars' chances for any kind of football tournament were all topics that could switch a conversation with speed.

"Exactly. It's not rocket science."

He laughed. "Not even close. Just logic."

A couple of minutes later, she reached the Allegiant Bank parking entrance, turned in, and pulled up in front of the first set of doors she saw.

Osei blasted her with a wide smile. "Thank you for the ride."

Her heart skipped a beat. It was as if he knew the power he held with those full lips.

"You're welcome. I'll be back tomorrow morning to work with your father. If your car isn't fixed, I could give you a ride."

Peace hovered in the invitation. She'd had a good time with him and wouldn't mind another chance at the experience. Besides, they'd be heading in the same direction tomorrow so she may as well be kind. It's how her mother had raised her to behave. *And has nothing to do with liking him.*

His brown eyes captured hers and held.

"I'd like that." He pointed to the fuel gauge. "I'll pay for petrol."

She arched a brow. The man kept surprising her, and she liked it. Apologies, questions, and an offer to pay for fuel all in thirty minutes had to be a record. Maybe he was worth getting to know better than she would during a short car ride.

Take a risk. He didn't have a wedding band on, and that sizzle when they'd touched had to mean something. *You'll never know if he likes you back until you go for it.*

"I'm good on petrol. How about if you take me out for lunch one day?"

Bold-as-brass was her new nickname. He wasn't the first man she'd ever asked out, but she'd never done it within hours of meeting. She knew very little about him, but she vibed with what she'd learned. Other than the arrogance, but that had disappeared quickly when he'd been humble enough to apologize.

Her stomach tightened with every passing second.

"That would be great," Osei finally said. "But between work and my father, I don't have a lot of time to spare these days."

The bottom of her car should've opened up and let her slither down to the concrete as her face got hot. Another first—and the rejection stung. She played it off with a shrug. "I understand. Have a good day. I'll see you tomorrow."

Or she'd have Daniel drag himself back and take the assignment. Knowing how unlikely that was to happen, she just hoped Osei would have left the house by the time she got there.

He lingered for a moment before lifting his bag onto his lap and reaching for the door handle. "Have a good day, Precious."

Unlikely, considering how she'd just humiliated herself.

Screeching tires would've been more satisfying than the careful manoeuvres she made to leave. What had gotten into her? She'd asked out a client. Technically, his father was her client, but still not something she usually did.

And he was an Ashanti man, of all people. What was she thinking to break her own rule of not getting involved with them? She'd maintained her peace of mind all of these years by abiding by it, only to be mortified when one had turned her down. Never again. No matter how handsome, interactive, successful, or caring to his family he was. Rules were meant to be kept. Lesson learned.

Taking deep, cleansing breaths, she imagined the situation happening in a different manner.

"*You don't have to worry about paying for petrol. It's not really out of my way,*" was what she should've said. As far as she was concerned, that's exactly how it had gone down.

The family had hired her for two sessions per day. With his work schedule, she wouldn't meet up with Osei during the late afternoon session, so she had a reprieve. If she saw him again tomorrow morning, the embarrassment could return then.

Chapter Four

"What's your view on the issue, Osei?" Ekow Adamani asked from his position at the head of the table.

Osei brought himself out of the memory of Precious' wide eyes filled with hurt as he'd declined her offer of lunch, into the meeting that should have been an e-mail. Good thing he hadn't spaced out completely. "It sounds like an effective plan, but I would recommend Christabella Oduro to lead the project. She has more experience and success when it comes to recruiting than Anthony."

Just like his boss did with him, Anthony, the HR department's laziest member, would foist the work to Christy, which would make her life harder. She may as well get the assignment straight away so she could offload whatever she was working on now. If his boss took less time to engage in company politics and paid more attention to his staff, he would've come to the same logical conclusion.

Ekow nodded in agreement. "You will oversee the project and ensure its success. Okay. On to the next item on the agenda."

Of course he would. Along with the other jobs that technically belonged to Ekow. If the promotion system hadn't been rotten to the core, Osei would've gotten the manager's job when they'd both applied for it. He'd been more qualified and had more longevity in the bank's HR department than his older colleague, but he hadn't known anyone at the top like Ekow had.

Now, he found himself working all the time at a job he no longer liked. Hated, in fact. Getting out of bed in the morning proved a struggle on the six, sometimes seven days of the week he had to work.

Then quit.

Easier said than done. Where else would he get a job that paid him at the level he was at now without placing even more pressure on him? Besides, who was hiring? In this economy, people were scrounging for jobs anywhere they could find it. Having one already, he'd be a fool to let it go.

He packed up his folder and tablet when the useless meeting ended.

"Osei, I want to talk to you for a moment," Ekow announced.

More work about to be piled onto his head. He wouldn't have it. Not now. He had his father to take care of, and for once, he wanted to be around to do his duty as a son.

Ekow waited until the conference room had cleared out. "Have you completed the monthly report? You should've turned it in by now so I can review it."

Meaning he'd send it in as his own work and give Osei none of the credit.

"It's almost done. I'll have it to you by three."

He wouldn't mention how busy and mentally preoccupied he'd been with his father. The man hadn't asked about him even once since Osei had initially told him about the stroke when it had occurred. Ekow's grunts and mumbles of people not working as hard as they should had fallen on uncaring ears when he'd left work early to go to the hospital. No one could've stopped him.

"Make sure you do." Ekow's voice had a warning tone to it. "Your appraisal is next week."

Irritated, Osei bit his tongue to keep in the insult. Despite Ekow's incompetence, he was still his boss. "Did you have anything else you wanted to discuss?"

"No."

Osei left the room and marched to his office. A lot smaller than Ekow's, but at least, he didn't have to share cubicle space with his co-workers. The enclosed area kept things private whenever someone came to complain or he had to deliver bad news.

He perused the report he'd finished last night on his laptop. Making Ekow sweat gave him a simple pleasure. It didn't make up for being overworked, but he found the positives of the job where he could. Despite the threat to his performance review, he may even hold out and send it to him tomorrow. A low, evil-type laugh bubbled out as he rubbed his hands together. Who said he wasn't fun?

Everyone.

Precious had been entertained enough by him to ask to spend more time with him. And he'd declined. Hours later, he still regretted it, but he'd told her the truth. He liked her and wanted to get to know her better, but he couldn't. The time not soaked up by his job was dedicated to helping his father get better and spending it with his family. He'd taken them for granted for too long. He had friends he needed to catch up with, too.

If his father's condition had taught him anything, it was that life is short and that the next day wasn't guaranteed. He vowed to live it with intentionality.

Going out with Precious would incur his father's wrath, and he refused to hinder his healing by going against his wishes. A shiver of dread slid down his spine as he considered life without the greatest man he'd ever known. No one would claim that Emmanuel Aboagye was perfect, but he had a caring heart, despite some of his stubborn ideologies. The man had educated himself to a Master's level, but when it came to some cultural aspects, he remained stuck in ancient times.

A pity his father refused to see that being human and loving each other proved more important than the tribe a person was from. The chair squeaked as he fell back into it, contemplating a different outcome for that morning. One where he'd be sitting across a table with Precious as they talked and laughed together. Maybe debated contentious issues, only to agree on others.

He huffed out a sigh. Overthinking the matter wouldn't help him feel better about having rejected her when he'd wanted to say yes. Opening a folder, he focused on the one thing that would keep Precious off his mind. Work.

***

All morning, the lurking heat of embarrassment had squirmed just beneath Precious' skin. Talking to her best friend on the phone wouldn't cut it. She'd texted Lamisi and set up a lunch meet. Even looking at the word *lunch* splashed her with mortification.

She arrived at Zora's Kitchen in Airport Residential area a few minutes earlier than planned and chose a seat on the veranda overlooking the lush backyard garden. They'd pre-ordered their meal online. In the mood for something comforting, she had gone for okra green soup with rice. As always, her friend would scoff at the non-traditional combination, but Precious loved it. Besides, she had to return to work, and eating banku or kenkey would be too heavy. She'd end up hiding in a corner of the hospital to sneak in a nap.

The ridiculousness of it made her smile.

"What has you so happy?"

She jumped up and hugged the woman she called a sister. Dr Lamisi Imoro, polyglot extraordinaire, squeezed her back.

"You look amazing," Precious gushed as they sat. "That new job with the American Embassy suits you."

"It's challenging, but I look forward to going into work. And…" Lamisi stretched out the word. "Legon offered me the position of Lecturer."

Ecstatic for her friend and all that she'd gone through to get to this point of having everything she wanted, Precious got up and hugged Lamisi again. "That's wonderful! Congratulations. They should've made you a full lecturer instead of an assistant the moment you stepped off the stage with your PhD. Next up is Professor."

"We all have to go through the bureaucratic process, no matter how frustrating it is." Lamisi patted the locs she'd started growing out a couple of months ago. "I reminded them I could only continue to work part-time, and they still wanted me."

"That's because your students love you, and they know it."

Lamisi lifted her chin and thrust her chest out. "It's because I'm fantastic."

Precious nodded at her friend's truth. "And oh, so humble about it, too."

"No need for humility when you have a gift like mine. Did I tell you that I'm learning Spanish now? I need to tap into the market the Spanish, Mexican, and South American embassies can provide."

"Soon, it's going to flow from you like water from a fountain."

She'd always been proud of Lamisi's ability to pick up languages. Despite that, from early in their friendship, they'd spontaneously decided to speak English together. It had helped Precious become more comfortable with the language used in the classroom when all she'd spoken at home was Ewe and then Twi at school with her classmates.

"What about Blaise's tour in June, will you be joining him this time?" Precious asked.

The hiplife artist had swept Lamisi off her feet and hadn't put her down since. Their story almost made Precious want the same thing. And then, she thought about her past. Pain proved a good reminder that long term relationships weren't for everyone.

"It's a shorter tour than the last one. He just wants to touch base with his Francophone fans so he stays in their sights until he comes out with his latest album which will drop in October."

Precious leaned forward with interest. Blaise was one of the hottest hiplife artists out there. When he'd started singing in French, his fame had quadrupled. "Will you help him translate his French songs again?"

A wide smile brightened Lamisi's face. "My husband is now fluent in the language and no longer needs my services to translate."

"Go, Blaise!" Precious said with a low hoot.

"He's worked hard to get where he is, and I'm proud of him." The glimmer in her eyes emphasized the sentiment.

The drinks and food arrived, and they started eating.

"What's going on?" Lamisi asked after a few forkfuls of her jollof rice and chicken.

With the rejection still painfully fresh, Precious needed Lamisi's reassurances that she hadn't made a massive mistake by putting herself out there and going for who she wanted. "I asked my client's son out on a date, and he said no."

"That bastard. Who does he think he is, turning down a wonderful woman like you? He has no idea what he's missing." She sucked her teeth hard. "Idiot."

Lamisi always knew what to say to pick her pride up from the floor. It didn't remove the shame of the experience, but it was good to hear that Osei was the loser in this situation, not her. She felt better already. "Thanks."

Lamisi waved down a hand. "Tell me who he is and what happened."

As they continued eating, she relayed the miserable tale ending with Osei's full name.

Good thing her friend had put her fork down and swallowed her food, because Lamisi's jaw dropped, revealing teeth, tongue, and tonsils. "Did you say his name is Osei Aboagye? Where is he from?"

Precious knew exactly where the conversation was going. "I'm not trying to marry him, just get to know him and have some fun. It's been a while since my *needs* were met."

"Avoiding my question is the answer. I can't believe you asked an Ashanti man out."

She stuffed her face with food to avoid replying.

Lamisi stared wide-eyed, her locs brushing her shoulders with the shake of her head. "You've sworn them all off, despite your father having been one."

Coming from two tribes with opposite lineage inheritance had left her alone when her parents had died. Traditionally, her father's tribe had a matrilineal inheritance, where the children belonged to the mother's side of the family, while her mother had been Ewe and they had a patrilineal inheritance. Aside from her parents having to fight their families to marry because neither wanted it to happen, the bigger issue had come when she'd been eight and the couple had died.

The lineal difference between the tribes had left her an orphan without anyone to claim her. Both families had refused, demanding it was the other's responsibility. If it hadn't been for her mother's best friend, she would've ended up on the streets or in an orphanage because no one had wanted her.

Precious drank from her glass in an attempt to push down the pain of the past. She missed her parents every day. Twenty-three years later, and neither of the families acknowledged her as theirs. Everything had turned out well for her only because of the woman she now called her mother.

Selorm Kpodo, an Ewe with the biggest heart in all of Ghana, became her new family. When she was twelve, Selorm adopted her, and Precious took her last name rather than keep her father's name of Gyasi. She'd cast off her Ashanti side and sworn off their men. No child of hers, if she ever had any, would ever experience the burden of being unwanted.

"I didn't mean to upset you."

Lamisi's soft voice dragged her from her past.

"I'm okay. Life is a series of lessons." She cleared her throat. "I should've stuck to my no Ashanti men mandate in the first place."

"Hmm. Do you remember what you used to tell me about my restrictive dating rules?"

Precious shook her head. "This is different. A child's life didn't hang in limbo if you hung on to yours. But me…"

"Precious, we're in the twenty-first century. I know that people still cling to tradition, but if you find the right man, regardless of his tribe, who comes from a loving and supportive family, then everything will work out." Lamisi grinned. "Besides, you know that your children are mine. They'll always be taken care of."

Her heart warmed at the sentiment of the words.

"I," Lamisi continued, "don't want you to miss out on love by blocking potential men."

Precious slumped as the humiliation returned. "You see what happened when I took a chance."

"Oh, please. You would've dumped him as soon as you really started to like him anyway."

Unable to argue with the assessment, Precious shrugged. She had deep-seeded issues she had no idea how to solve. Didn't know if she even wanted to. Staying isolated had kept her from getting hurt. That was all she wanted out of life, to keep the agony of loss away.

That's depressing. She wouldn't have her aunt forever. Her friends were wonderful, but she couldn't expect them to always be around when they had their own lives to experience. If she kept on the same path, she'd end up not only alone, but lonely.

"Good job for asking this stupid Osei guy out," Lamisi said. "You liked what you saw, despite him being Ashanti. It's progress that I hope will grow."

Osei's grinning face came to mind. Once he'd put the phone down while she drove, their conversation had flowed. She'd enjoyed that. And he had an established career, despite him not liking his job. She held back a sigh at what had impressed her most about him. He'd asked about her rather than rambling on about himself and had actually been interested in what she'd had to say.

That's what had made her ask him out. A little bit of attention from a man who made her stomach wobble, her heart race, and her mouth go dry, and now, she found herself swimming in a pool of regret.

Chapter Five

If Osei packed up his things and left the house right then, he'd arrive at work an hour and a half early. It wouldn't be a total loss because he had assignments to catch up. Despite major efforts to focus yesterday, his thoughts had kept ricocheting back to the time he'd spent with Precious. And the inevitable way their conversation had ended.

Knowing his father wouldn't accept her as anything more than his physiotherapist had driven him to deny what he'd wanted. To get to know her better. Kiss those supple lips. Caress her smooth, rich brown skin. A tingle raced down his spine just thinking about it. How much better would it be in actuality?

Tossing wisdom away, he went to the hall where he'd wheeled his father in his recliner after he'd helped him take care of his bathroom necessities and got him ready for the day. The activities hadn't been as difficult as he'd initially anticipated. Seeing his hero struck down with illness had crushed him, but he was grateful for his father's survival.

They'd spent the time talking. Not the functional kind of conversations they tended to have about the family and politics—more of a getting to know each other session. Something they didn't do regularly because Osei was rarely home. It had been a positive experience he looked forward to repeating until his father became strong enough to care for himself and beyond.

He sat on the end of the couch closest to where his father watched the news.

"Enoch Dzamesi has been appointed by the president as the latest Justice of the Supreme Court," the news anchor announced just before showing a video of the judge celebrating with his friends, family, and supporters.

Osei's skin stretched over clenched muscles as he listened, waiting for his father's reaction to the announcement.

"You see, right there!" His father pointed a finger at the screen as he spoke in Twi. "Another Ewe in a high position. Did you know that out of the nine posts on the supreme court, three of them are held by Ewes? With their constant education and always looking out solely for themselves, if we don't take care, they're likely to fill all of the important jobs in Ghana. Where would that leave the rest of us?"

Osei broke eye contact as his father pinned him with a gaze that demanded an answer. "But this judge is the same political party as you. Does it matter what tribe he's from, as long as he gets the job done?"

His father grumbled. "Sometimes, politics is more than affiliation. They take care of their own too much, so why can't Akans do the same? If they don't, then Ewes will take over the country and drive it into the gutter. If we aren't vigilant, the capital will be moved to the Volta Region or some nonsense like that."

Osei's stomach quivered at the sentiment his father had spouted since he'd been a child. He had no ill feelings about any other tribe. It had always been the Ewes that his father had never cared for as a people.

"But you work with them," Osei spoke up. "And some of your students are Ewe. They're no worse or better than people from any other tribe."

If it hadn't been for his mother, would he have fallen into the trap of not liking an ethnic group?

"Don't let them fool you like they did me, son. It's necessary to work with them because they're everywhere. For the sake of a peaceful workplace, I'm cordial, but I will always recognize them for the potential of treachery they're capable of. They take everything and give nothing in return but strife."

His father shook his head. "This is why when I discovered that your fool-hearty brother was dating one, I put a stop to it immediately. No Ewe will ever infiltrate my family. My uncle warned me, and I didn't listen until it was too late."

Osei swallowed, torn between defending a tribe of people and asking his father point blank about what had brought on his hatred of the Ewes. He'd once mentioned an incident that had occurred when he was younger where his life had been placed in danger, but hadn't expounded. He'd merely warned his children to keep Ewes at arm's length and to never turn their back on them.

His father's keen eyes met his. "Are you heading to work?"

At the sharp change in topic, he'd lost his opportunity to delve further into his father's past. *For now.* "I thought I'd stick around and see if Precious needs any help since no one else is around."

His mother had left earlier to get some shopping done and to check on the inventory of her beverage shop. Osei had told Dorcas he would assist with today's physiotherapy session. Since she was on long break from university, she'd take over being with their father when he left.

His father looked at him for a length of time that would've had him shifting in his seat if he hadn't caught on long ago about the discomfort of silence. He often used the technique with his colleagues to get them to open up, and sometimes confess.

Osei held his tongue. What would he say? That he wanted to see Precious again because even after just a couple of hours, he'd known he liked her? His family had been all over her when she'd arrived yesterday— they already knew how special she was. His turn now.

His father broke the silence. "Yesterday afternoon, she mentioned we would do longer durations of standing and try walking today. It might be good to have you around."

The shrill sound of the ringer at the gate registered, and Osei shot to his feet, reminding himself not to run as he headed to the door. Before unlocking the pathway gate, he twisted the kinks out of his neck to calm his excitement, despite anticipating the attitude she'd throw at him.

Did he deserve it? Better to spare them both than to pursue an ill-fated attraction. Yet, he'd stayed rather than scurry off to work to avoid her. Foolishness never ended well.

When he opened the gate, the space was empty. Stepping out, he found his gaze landing on Precious' round behind as she reached into the back of her car. He was still ogling her when she stood and turned with her arms full of what looked like railings.

Caught, he snapped his attention to her face where he anticipated a stern, annoyed expression. Instead, her lips were slightly open and her eyes wide as their gazes linked and held for several seconds. He stood captivated. Not even the haziness of the light Harmattan fog could dim her beauty.

"Good morning, Osei."

Her voice came out huskier than he remembered it from yesterday.

"Good morning, Precious." He'd spoken already that morning, so his own voice shouldn't have been as raspy as it sounded. What about her made him feel as if he were a teenager trying to gain control of his body and will? He regretted not being able to discover if they could've had something special. Clearing his throat, he moved forward and reached out for what she held. "Can I help you with that?"

"Oh. Yes. They aren't heavy, just a little bulky."

When he reached for them, his hand landed over hers. A pleasant sting of electricity bit into his flesh, and he let the touch linger as their eyes held steady. Her chest rose and fell with fast breaths while his heart raced. His lips throbbed with the need to kiss her. Just one would appease the fantasy that had replayed in his mind all night.

She pulled her hand from beneath his and jerked her head to look inside her car. "You can go ahead. I'll bring in the rest of the things."

Now that he'd seen her again, it proved a struggle to leave her side, so he watched until she'd pulled a duffle bag from the vehicle and closed the hatch. While carrying the two items she'd given him in one hand, he reached for the bag with his free hand.

"I can carry it," she said.

"It's the gentlemanly thing to do. My parents would expect no less."

She huffed out a breath and handed it over.

His arm dipped at the unexpected weight of the bag before he recovered and swung it onto his shoulder. "After you."

A light floral scent tinged with lemon and cocoa butter that he would forever recognize as hers tantalized as she passed by. Enticement now went by the name of Precious, and he needed to stay away.

***

"Your father is a determined man," Precious said as she settled into the vehicle with Osei in the passenger's seat.

Taking off, she drove down the uncongested, well-maintained roads of Cantonment residential area. The fervent prayers she'd made that Osei wouldn't be around that morning hadn't been answered. The moment she'd caught him staring at her, the extreme mortification she'd expected had left. There'd been a magnetic draw to him as their gazes held. She realized she would've regretted not asking him out a lot more than she did being rejected. A pride in her courage to take a chance overshadowed the risk, but it still stung.

Despite how much she'd attempted to give Mr Aboagye her full attention, it had been unevenly split between the Aboagye men. Osei had made his broad-shouldered presence known in her periphery, his fresh scent wafting around her when he came near, and his deliciously deep voice humming in her ear the few times he'd spoken.

Every time she'd looked at him, her stomach had quivered, overshadowing the tinge of embarrassment that still lingered. She was sure he felt it, too. Whenever they touched, his gaze flew to hers, and the dark pupils in his clear brown eyes dilated the slightest bit. Still, nothing she could do about it. His rebuff wouldn't hit her twice.

"He's always been stubborn," Osei replied. "He came from a farming family of twelve in Mpasaso."

"I've never been there, but my—" she cut herself off from talking about her father's family. She'd given up speaking about both sides when they'd tossed her away without a single thought for how she'd survive. "I know people from Beposo. I travelled there a few times when I was younger. Did your father come from rich cocoa farmers?"

"Ha. Not if you hear the story from him. Dirt poor. His parents could barely make ends meet. He couldn't even dream of getting the things his friends came to school with, but he states with pride that they never went to bed hungry."

Precious held back the jealousy at the thought of having eleven brothers and sisters. She'd have been happy with one. "Were your grandparents able to send all of them to school?"

For her, the most important aspect of being a parent meant the ability to provide the basics for the children, and to ensure they became more than their parents were. That showed love, not just a sense of responsibility.

Osei's brows crinkled together. "I've never asked. The majority of my aunts and uncles are still in Mpasaso. I had always presumed they were farming. My father and his twin sisters came to Accra when they were sixteen and fifteen."

Kayayo, the young girls hired to carry items in the market areas of large cities, came to mind. A difficult life. "They skipped straight over Kumasi, then?"

"My father had a brother who lived in Accra and had invited three of my father's children to help him with his poultry business here."

Precious nodded. "The devil you know is better than the angel you don't."

He made a clicking sound in his throat. "I detest that saying. If I'd been the one to choose, I would've been like my father and taken a chance with an angel any day."

She dipped her head to the side in interest, wanting to ask him why he hadn't taken a chance with her. But then, she remembered the logic that had weaved answers into her brain last night. Despite how he watched her when he thought she wasn't aware, he may have a girlfriend, even a wife overseas. She could accept that. It made her respect him.

Now stalled in traffic, she turned to face him. "I agree, but it's how many people think. It keeps them in the known rather than venturing out into new territory where they're afraid to go in the first place."

Their eyes locked. She could see the wheels turning. "What are you thinking?"

He shook his head slightly and looked away. "Fear keeps us from doing everything we want to do in life."

The snort burst out from her. "That, and listening to the advice of other people when you tell them your plans. Which is also based on fear."

"And envy," he added.

"PHD," they said at the same time and laughed. The pull her/him down syndrome was a real thing in Ghana. Crabs in a bucket had nothing on them when trying to escape the harshness of their lives. Instead of supporting a person so they could make it out and do better for themselves, the misery they were in had to be shared, so they'd hinder anyone who tried.

She inched the car forward. "Since your father ended up being a headmaster of a predominant secondary school here in Accra, I take it the chance he took on himself paid off."

"He said it wasn't easy, and if he hadn't met our mother, he may not have been as successful."

She touched her chest. "That's so sweet."

Osei clasped his hands together on his lap and rolled his thumbs. "Once he knows what he wants, he perseveres towards it. Dada's desire right now is to be independent and not rely on his family to help him do basic things like going to the toilet, so that's what will happen."

"Good. Those are the kind of clients with the best outcomes. Look how long he stood without support. And those steps he took were impressive. We just need to increase his strength, and he'll be doing it all on his own."

"I'm relieved to hear you confirm it."

Osei's smile competed with the sunlight spraying through the clouds overhead. She could stare at it all day. She fought to look back at the road as her heart clenched at what would never be.

"I'm getting my car back today," he announced.

She pressed her lips together in disappointment. No matter what had happened yesterday, it was easy to be around him, and she'd been hoping to at least spend the next two workdays as his transporter. Maybe she'd see him when she came to work with his father in the mornings.

Not the same. After experiencing professional guilt for not giving Mr Aboagye a hundred percent of her attention, a part of her hoped Osei wouldn't be around for the sessions. Maybe then, she'd stop liking him.

"That's good," she lied. "What kind of car do you drive?" *Probably something that fit his room-filling persona, like a Hummer in the biggest size it came.*

"An Audi A4."

A luxury sedan. Interesting. Work hard, play harder kind of car. In her case, work hard, save hard. She had a business to get up and running, and spending her money on a dream car wouldn't get her there. Once she'd reached her goal, she'd be free to get whatever she wanted, within reason.

They spent the rest of the journey discussing the difficulty of dealing with mechanics in Accra. When they reached his building, she didn't want him to go, but darned if she'd ever ask him out again.

"Thank you for the ride."

"You're welcome." In order to mentally prepare herself, she asked, "Will I see you tomorrow morning?"

If she hadn't been watching him so carefully, she'd have missed the slight wince.

"No. I need to get into work earlier than usual to complete a project."

Two days. They'd known each other for a few hours, and yet, her chest tightened in response to not seeing him again. Ridiculous. She pasted on a smile. "Have a good day and take care."

He opened his mouth then closed it before reaching for the door handle. "Thank you, Precious."

Climbing out, he closed the door and gave her a wave while waiting for her to take off.

"Okay, girl," she mumbled to herself as she drove away. "Now you know Mr Osei Aboagye, fine boy extraordinaire, isn't for you. Men aren't your focus anyway. Starting a rehab centre is. Stay on track."

However, the speech didn't take away the sense of loss. With the relationships she'd had, she hadn't taken the fall. Not like Lamisi who had founds someone to commit to and was happy. She wanted the kind of supportive, passionate, joy-inducing relationship her friend had. When would love be hers? Not that she'd expected Osei to be the love of her life, but she was ready for it. She could fall in love and run a business at the same time.

Just not with Osei.

Chapter Six

"When was the last time we came to the market?" Precious asked as she skirted out the way of a giggling little boy with blond hair who ran past her as a young woman tagged after him.

She'd missed the open friendliness of the monthly market. This was one of the best places to find handmade quality products which were often sold by the creators themselves at this purchasing ground for Ghanaians and expats alike. She hadn't discovered it until her friend had opened her eyes to the experience.

"You mean, how long since you've gotten a dozen bagels to wolf down in four days?" Toyin said with an arched brow. "At least five months."

Offended, she gasped. "It takes me longer than that to eat all those bagels."

Toyin looked her up, down, and back up again. "Call me a liar all you want, but I know what I know."

She frowned at the snippiness in his tone. "What's wrong? You've been acting out of sorts since you picked me up."

Her friend let out a long-suffering sigh as he shifted to his other foot. "I'm nervous."

"About?" She dragged the word out, wishing they could skip the drama, get to the point, and head over to her bagel guy. Sobolo was calling out to her, too. One of the many sellers of the hibiscus drink made the best she'd ever tasted.

Toyin leaned in a little closer. "I should've told you, but do you remember the guy I've been talking to for the past few months?"

"You mean Gideon? The expat who works for a gold mine and hasn't been in a relationship for over a year because the man he was seeing broke it off without telling him. Do you mean that guy?"

"You're such a smart ass. Yes, him. We agreed to meet here."

Precious slid him a side eye emphasized with a twist of her lips. "Toyin! You asked me to come here today so we could hang out, and now, you're going to ditch me when Gideon comes around? That's wrong."

"No, girl. That's strategic. You know I won't leave you. I drove, remember? I wanted you as a buffer."

"To use me." Hard to keep up the annoyed act when she was happy for her friend finally getting to meet the man he'd been raving about.

Toyin bit his lower lip. "Not at all. You've been whining about missing those bagels, so I thought I'd treat you."

She placed a hand on her hip and dipped her head to the side, playing it out for as much as she could get. "You want me to be a third wheel for a dozen bagels?"

"Fine, add that cold pressed coconut oil you like so much."

"I'm getting the biggest bottle they have." She scanned the crowded marketplace. "Do you see him?"

"No. We said we'd meet at eleven. Fifteen minutes to go. Let's get your extortion bagels."

She laughed at her Nigerian friend's accusation. They'd hit it off the first time they'd met six years ago at a book club after hating the book the rest of the group had loved. He'd made her laugh with his comments about the story, and they'd been tight ever since. The best part was that Lamisi had also gotten along with him so they hung out together often.

Content with her bagels and bottle of coconut oil in the shopping bag slung over her shoulder, she chewed on the free bagel given to her as she washed it down with the sweet Sobolo. They didn't stop at any other sellers as they headed to the front gate where Gideon and Toyin had agreed to meet.

This wasn't the first time Toyin had dragged her out on a date with him. With many Ghanaians being vicious towards the LGBTQ+ community, Toyin was uneasy about who he'd meet. She didn't mind joining him. The romantic in her loved watching the sparks fly when they happened, and dragging him out of the situation when they didn't. Her wing woman skills were extraordinary. Lamisi and Blaise could attest to that. Them getting together had been all her, regardless of how Lamisi told the story.

She suddenly caught sight of a familiar profile and stopped in the middle of the pathway. Was that…? No, it couldn't be. He'd said he was too busy working to enjoy life. The way Osei was animatedly speaking to a couple holding hands before bursting into laughter could define having a good time.

Her breath hitched as her eyes roved over his strong physique covered with a bright wax print the opposite of the conservative shirt and tie combo she'd seen him in three days ago. It seemed like half a century had passed.

"What's he doing here?"

"Who?" Toyin asked while craning his neck.

She stepped off the path and pretended to view some silver jewellery. "Don't make it obvious, but one of my client's children is five tables down on the right."

Toyin took a covert peek. "Do you mean that fine boy with all that wood?" He giggled.

At any other time, the pun would've made her laugh, but she remained stone-faced as her stomach tightened and her mind calculated how long it would take to get to the back exit.

"Come on, Precious. Considering what's surrounding him, you have to admit that was a good one."

"Ha ha ha."

"Why are you hiding from him?"

She gave the jewellery seller a polite nod and stepped behind her table into a small space where she was sure Osei couldn't see her without looking behind him. "I sort of accidentally asked him out on a lunch date a few days ago."

Toyin nodded. "And now, he won't leave you alone. Say no more. We'll go to the back and walk around to meet up with Gideon."

She resisted the urge to fling her arms around her friend. "Actually…" Her hands felt cool as she pressed them against her cheeks, heated with resumed humiliation. "He turned me down."

Toyin's mouth went slack before his lips tensed and his eyes narrowed. He rotated on the heel of his custom-made leather sandal and headed in Osei's direction.

Precious caught his arm before he could get more than a few feet away. Hard muscles tensed under her hand. She positioned herself to face him. "Where are you going?"

"To tell him about himself. No one—" he held up an index finger, "—and I mean no one, says no when you ask them out. Girl, you're fabulous, and he needs to know what he missed out on. I'm going to inform him of his major mistake, live and in person."

Toyin's unbridled support meant the world to her, but now wasn't the time to get sentimental. "I'm sure he had a good reason. He might have a girlfriend or may even be married. Maybe he's gay."

He sucked his teeth as he rolled his eyes. "Nonsense. You have an uncanny gift for figuring out who's attached or not. Why do you think I always have you tag along on my first dates?"

One of her skills was assessing people, and she was rarely wrong. Yet, that very rarity tended to catch her off guard and set her on her behind. She looped an arm through his and attempted to lead him towards the back of the market. "Speaking of which, you have a man to meet and dump me for like you always do."

Toyin couldn't resist any topic about him. "I can't help it if you decline to join us once you give me the thumbs up." He waved a hand and caught the air in front of his face. "You won't distract me from my mission of telling that jerk off. No."

"Precious? I thought that was you."

She froze as her heart raced. Back stiff, she glanced up at Toyin and gave him a sharp shake of her head. He must've interpreted the scowl she threw at him as the *I-will-neuter-you-if-you-say-anything* message she'd intended because he mouthed, *fine*.

As a unit, they turned, Toyin with a slight snarl and her with her breath smelling like the garlic and onion bagel she'd just devoured.

"Yes, it's me. Hi, Osei."

Chapter Seven

The odds of meeting up with Precious at the monthly Blue Leaf Market, a popular spot in Accra for those looking for a light, friendly atmosphere to buy crafted items weren't astronomical, but Osei was pleasantly surprised. His gaze skipped from Precious to the man standing next to her, leaving him stumped for a moment. Was she on a date?

None of his business. He battled the overwhelming need to step in between the two and turn his back on the light-skinned, copper-haired man who had a full head of height on Osei's five-foot-eleven frame and possessed a lot more muscle.

Straightening, he nodded at her escort in recognition before returning his attention to her. "How are you?"

She graced him with a small smile. "I'm well, thanks. How are you?"

He'd been better when she'd dropped him off at work. The decision he'd made to avoid her at all costs had been difficult to maintain when he knew she'd be in his home. Leaving early had kept him from seeing her, but not from missing her. "I'm also doing well. Thank you."

The awkwardness of the encounter stretched for several seconds as his mind scrounged for something to add.

Precious waved towards her companion. "This is Toyin Awolowo. Toyin, this is my client's son, Osei Aboagye."

Osei held back a grimace at the description she'd given him as he offered a hand. Toyin grabbed it and squeezed. Hard.

He returned the painful pressure. "Hello. *O dara lati pade yin Toyin.*"

The other man's grip relaxed as his grin revealed a joyful surprise at hearing that it was nice to meet him in what, from his name, Osei had presumed to be his native language.

"You speak Yoruba?" Toyin asked in his mother tongue.

Osei took his hand back and kept it at his side without pumping it to return the circulation. "A few words," he said in English. "I've travelled to Lagos many times for trainings. One of my proud Yoruba colleagues from there was called Olutoyin."

Toyin's earlier animosity left as he tapped his chest. "That's my full name, too, but only my mother uses it," he said with a chuckle. "It's good to meet you, Osei."

"We were heading off to meet someone," Precious said. "It was nice seeing you again."

He couldn't let this chance encounter pass so quickly when she'd been so heavily on his mind. "You can at least visit my booth."

Her brows raised. "*You're* selling something here?"

Rather than explain, he led them to an area where he sold his reclaimed wood products. He stood with anticipation as they looked at his handmade tables, mirrors, chopping boards, coasters, and more. Anything his mind could think to create with the wood he salvaged.

"Osei," Precious breathed out. "These are beautiful."

His chest swelled with the pride of his work. "Thank you."

The young man he'd hired as an assistant for market days dealt with the other potential customers, allowing him to focus on her.

She shuffled through the loose wooden coasters inlaid with varying wax print and Kente designs. Her eyes lit up when she saw a triple-layered floor stand. "Oh, my goodness, Toyin. This would be perfect in the hall."

Toyin, tapping on his phone, looked up. "Next to the side of the couch."

Osei's head jerked back at the realization of how well they knew each other. Were they lovers? If so, had her invitation to lunch just been something friendly? No. He hadn't gotten that vibe from her when her eyes had widened and her lips had pouted the slightest as she'd waited for his answer.

"Exactly!" she exclaimed.

As she continued to assess the piece, Osei attempted to appease his mounting curiosity. "How do you two know each other?"

That sounded jealous as hell when it came out in a harsher tone than he'd intended. He added a smile to soften the question.

Toyin was the only one to react as his head tilted to the side.

"Look at this, Toyin," Precious said with excitement as she showed him a nested serving tray with a purple, gold, and white wax print inlay.

Toyin went closer and touched the piece. "Your favourite colour combo."

Osei ground his teeth, his jaw tightening with the elevated level of envy he shouldn't be experiencing. He had no right to it. He and Precious barely knew each other, and because of his father's tribal bias, he couldn't indulge in the attraction he'd discovered with her. And still he fumed.

Precious held onto the tray as she continued to peruse the other items.

"We met at a book club years ago," Toyin said. "We've been fast *friends* ever since."

Osei relaxed at the dropped hint, feeling as if he'd made an ally in the other man. "Are you still in the book club?"

"We meet once a month at a member's house in Madina," Toyin answered. "We read books from all over the world, different genres so it broadens the mind. It's a lot of fun and a great way to meet people. Or get to know someone better. You should join us. You can bring your S-O if you want."

"S-O?"

"Significant other," Toyin clarified.

Osei's eyes flicked to Precious who had returned to looking through the coasters and had four in the serving tray she'd been guarding.

He sighed, wishing things could've been different between them. "I don't have anyone, so it would just be me."

"Precious, I should get some kind of commission for bringing people into the book club. We've recruited ourselves a new member."

Her eyes went wide. One of the coasters slipped from her hand and onto the grass. She bent to pick it up, and when she returned to standing, the shocked expression had disappeared.

"With your long hours at the bank and—" She raised a palm skyward and did a slow slide wave over his products as if presenting something exquisite, "—creating all of this, will you have time to read?"

"I'm a fast reader. As long as the book isn't voluminous and intense, it should be fine."

She nodded, her lips tilted into a frown. Was she thinking about the excuse he'd given for declining her lunch date offer? He hadn't found time for seeing her, but he was willing to make some for reading a book? He rubbed the back of his neck, feeling guilty about the turn of events.

"Are you definitely coming?" Toyin raised a hand. "I vote yes."

He wanted to be around her without getting to like her too much. They could meet in the friendship zone. Discussing books was an impersonal way of hanging out and seeing if they could become friends.

"Sure. I'll give it a trial run. What's the book, and when is the next meeting?"

"Great." Toyin said. "We all buy our books from Georgina, the head of the club, but because this is so last minute, you can get your own. The meeting is next week, Friday. Precious will send you the details."

She shot Toyin a look that should've sliced him in half. "Um, sure."

They exchanged numbers, the interaction making him happy while Precious seemed hesitant. He couldn't blame her after his behaviour. "Have you decided to purchase anything?"

"Yes. I'll take these." She held out her items. "And the stand. Will it fit in your car, Toyin?"

"Only if I drive with my knees in my chest."

She giggled. "I'd pay to see that. Where do you store the pieces, Osei?"

Once again, he became uncomfortably aware of their relationship. They may not be lovers, but the two were close. His gut twisted. Truth be told, it's what he wanted with her. Yet, the consequences were too steep to ever allow it. "We have a garage on my parents' property that I use as a work space."

"That's perfect. If it's okay, I'll pick it up on Monday when I stop by."

"And leave it in your car while you're at work? Doesn't sound safe to me." Toyin chimed in before Osei could get the chance.

"It's quality furniture, not a laptop computer covered in cash," she retorted.

"You don't need your car broken into," Osei said. "How about if I drop it off to you?"

Toyin gave a single nod of approval. "That's a great idea. You mentioned that you're going to be home all evening. What time would you be able to drop it off?"

She tapped the serving tray and glowered at her friend. "You can't volunteer someone, Toyin." She shifted her gaze to Osei. "You probably have plans. If you keep it in your parents' place, I'll pick it up when I come for the evening session on Monday."

Anticipation stirred in him at getting to see her tonight. Maybe spend some time with her. Everything in him pushed to make it happen while he could. "And leave you without this one-of-a-kind furniture that will become the talking piece of your hall? Not a chance. I'm a better businessman than that. How about I stop by at around six?"

"That's perfect. She'll see you then." Toyin closed the deal. "Now let's pay for the things so we can make my appointment. I've already postponed it by fifteen minutes, and I don't want to risk missing it."

Osei had secretly hoped to see Precious as he'd started his day, but this was beyond what he'd expected and he actually felt giddy. "Because you're helping my father to be independent again, I'll give you a discount."

When he told her the new price of the items, her mouth rounded.

"That isn't good business, Osei. I can't pay that, not when you're also delivering."

He would have given her the items for free if he didn't have a sense she'd decline. "I'm also remembering the rides you graciously gave me."

"She accepts. She'll text you her address. Now, pay him and let's go," Toyin insisted.

Within two minutes, Osei watched them walk towards the front entrance. Precious turned and looked over her shoulder to find him staring. The smile and wave seemed to happen in slow motion, and his heart responded with a sudden jerk.

They'd be friends.
With no benefits.
He shook his head.

Absolutely no benefits.

Chapter Eight

The butterflies in Precious' stomach refused to take a break. Six-fifteen already, and Osei hadn't shown up. Maybe he'd changed his mind, and she'd soon receive a text that would make her feel lower than low.

Her conversation with Toyin as they'd waited for the man she now considered to be a perfect match for him had been enlightening.

"What was all that about?" she'd asked. "One minute, you want to tell him off, and the next, you're setting us up."

"Osei likes you."

She'd craned her neck forward as if that would give her a better understanding. "What makes you say that?"

"I could tell by the way he looked at you. And if we lived in a more violent kind of society, he might have gone off on me in a fit of jealousy."

Her brows had raised in confusion. "I don't believe it. He has nothing to be jealous of."

"Pardon? Look at me." The full circle he'd made with his arms outstretched had been dramatically presented. "I'm magnificent. A catch of whale-sized proportions. I'm—"

She'd rolled her eyes. "What I meant was he doesn't care about me. We barely know each other. And he declined my invitation. Remember?"

"Trust me when I say he likes you. And by the way, he's as hetero as they come. When have I ever been wrong—"

She'd flung up a finger, ready to give specific examples when he'd caught her hand.

"In regards to other people. I'm a mess at figuring things out for myself." He'd squeezed the hand he still held. "That's why I have you. There's no wasting time with you vetting my guys."

Before she could dive further into the topic of Osei, the tall, handsome, dark-haired, tanned Caucasian man she'd recognized from the pictures Toyin had gushed over walked towards them. Gideon's striking blue eyes focused on her friend with an adoration no one had ever thrown in her direction.

After a brief conversation, they'd left the market and gone out for lunch. By the end of the meal, Precious had known without a doubt that if neither of the men let fear get in the way, they'd be very happy together. Since Gideon had taken a taxi to meet them, he'd tagged along when Toyin gave her a ride home, so there'd been no further insights about Osei.

Now, she sat alone in the hall of her apartment in Adjiringanor. Fresh from a shower, she wore a cute light green linen dress that ended just above the knees and had spritzed on her favourite lemon and gardenia perfume. She'd even taken her hair out of her perpetual bun and let it lay to its full relaxed length brushing the tops of her shoulders.

If he didn't arrive soon, she'd head over to her mother's chop bar and hang out there. She looked too good to sit alone all-night ruminating about how wrong Toyin had been about Osei.

The chime of her doorbell had her jumping off the couch and running to the intercom. "Who is it?"

"Osei Aboagye. I'm here with your stand."

She extended her arms to her sides and huffed out a breath. This was a furniture delivery. That's all. "I'll be down in a minute."

She took her time descending the two flights of stairs. When she opened the door, her heart thumped hard before it started racing at the sight of Osei in a brown and white wax print shirt over tan trousers he'd changed into. Her spirts plummeted at the realization he must be going out after the delivery because he looked too good to just be heading back home. A date?

She wrestled with the jealousy that had come out of nowhere. He had the right to have a good time, even if it was without her.

"Hi, Osei."

"Good evening. Sorry I'm late."

"That's okay. I'm grateful you could drop it off." She looked down at the piece and fell in love all over again at the spectacular craftsmanship. She'd never seen anything like it before. The pseudo rounded shapes of the three varying sizes of wood gleamed as it caught the light.

"Do you need help carrying it up? I live on the second floor. No elevators."

"I can handle it."

The cuff of his short-sleeved shirt strained against the bulge of his muscles when he lifted the stand. He must do more than work behind a desk to have such definition.

Realizing she was gawking, she pivoted and took the lead up the stairs. When they'd reached her apartment, she was slightly out of breath, but not due to physical exertion. She'd never felt like this before, and she barely knew him. It had to be the novelty of him that set her body off. The next time she saw him, she'd be…normal.

Opening the door, she stepped out of the way to let him in.

"Where do you want it?"

She swallowed hard as an image of them naked, skin glistening with sweat with him on top of her in bed, filled her head. What was wrong with her? "Next to the couch, please."

He bent at the knees and lowered the piece.

Assessing the room, she frowned. "It doesn't seem right."

Osei rotated and took in the hall. "It's more of a stand-alone piece. The couch crowds it. How about a few feet away from the flat screen?"

She considered the idea knowing very well home décor wasn't her specialty. "Let's try it."

With ease, he moved the furniture to where he'd suggested.

"It's still not right." Maybe the corner closest to the door would be better. She could envision some plants cascading over it. Feeling bad about him having to do so much work, she waved a hand. "I'll move it later. Would you like some water?"

"Yes, but tell me where you want this. I don't mind." He chuckled. "My mother has often had me move a piece of furniture several times only to settle it in the original spot."

"Sounds like me. Change isn't really my thing, even though I say I may want it initially. Three years living in the same place and I've added to it, but not shifted anything."

She thought of Lamisi who was ready and willing to move furniture around on a monthly basis if it struck her. *Perhaps that's why she's reached her goals, and I'm still trying to achieve mine.* The revealing thought sent a shiver down her spine. She'd have to analyse it later.

"Change can be difficult, but when you're happy with the result, it's worth it." His eyes connected with hers and held.

He wasn't talking about furniture anymore. The vibes pulsing from him made her mouth dry and her nipples tighten. If it had been any other man she'd wanted to get to know making her feel as if her body were vibrating, she'd have initiated a move that would have him kissing her. But this was the guy who had turned her down. She wouldn't take that risk again.

She stepped back towards the kitchen on the other side of the open-plan room. "I'm—" she cleared her throat. "I'm going to get some water. Have a seat."

In the kitchen, she wiped her moist palms on the dish cloth hanging on the oven handle as she sucked in several breaths to calm herself. Her imagination wasn't good enough to have created the longing intensity in his eyes. Toyin was right. He wanted her. What was holding him back?

Grabbing two sachets of water, she placed them and a glass on her brand-new tray. She'd get one for her mother. Lamisi would love one, too.

In the hall, she held out the tray to offer him the water.

"Thank you." He took a sachet, but left the glass on the tray.

She sat in the loveseat opposite him, snipped off a piece of plastic with her teeth, and took a long sip to hopefully cool the desire warming low in her belly. "I can't equate the serious Type A human resource manager with the woodworker."

"I'm not always serious."

She shot him a side eye yeah-right look that made him laugh.

He downed the water in a few gulps and placed the plastic on the tray. "My job is stressful, and working with reclaimed wood is how I relax."

Intrigued, she hinged forward. "How did you get into it?"

"My cousin attended vocational school where he learned how to make furniture. I was visiting one day while he was creating, and he taught me some of what he knew. I enjoy working with my hands, and with practice, I became better. In the beginning, I distributed them as gifts to friends and family."

Intrigued, she recalled a piece she'd seen in his home. "Did you make the dining room table in your parents' house?"

His head jerked back, as he seemed surprised she'd noticed his handiwork. "It was an anniversary gift. My mother was ecstatic. My father told me I'd done a good job with it, but I should focus on making my way up the ladder at work."

It sounded like the focused man she'd come to know. "That must've been disappointing. I'm sure it would be a great business for you to go into full-time."

He clasped his hands over his flat stomach. "When my job gets to me, I think about it. A lot. But this trade won't pay into my retirement."

The words deflected as a fear of branching out on his own. She hated for people to give up on their dreams. "Being in HR, you know you could contribute to your social security account yourself. Your work is fabulous, and with the right marketing strategy, I'm sure you'd make more than enough to support yourself and your future."

Osei shook his head. "It's not the direction I'm headed in. For now, I'm happy to work on it as a hobby, sell at markets, and deliver my pieces to damsels in furniture arranging distress."

She chuckled. "That's one way of putting it."

He raised a finger to the ceiling. "Before I leave, this stand will be in a place that will make you content."

This playful side of Osei surprised and encouraged her. She sprung to her feet. "Challenge accepted. As long as you continue to do the heavy lifting."

He stood and flexed his arms with a grunt. "Of course. I'll even contribute with a few decorating tips that I've learned over the years."

"Now you're just showing off, but let's get to it."

Twenty minutes later, every piece of furniture in her hall sat in a completely different place. The stand ended up next to the couch as she'd anticipated, only in another spot of the room. His suggestions had been brilliant. They'd joked and laughed the whole time, revealing how fun he could be. A trait she loved in a man.

She'd fallen into a deeper state of admiration with Osei than she'd been in before.

Futile and dangerous.

Chapter Nine

"Was that your stomach or mine?" Osei asked once they'd completed the task of setting her hall up in way that flowed better than before.

"You don't ask that of a woman. It's indelicate." The teasing sparkle in her eyes eased the chastisement.

From the way she'd interacted with his family, he knew she was enjoyable to be around, but experiencing it first-hand was something he wanted to continue. "My mother never taught us that. I know never to ask a woman's age and when she's expecting to deliver if she looks pregnant. I learned the hard way she might not be."

"Oh, no," she said with a giggle. "That must've been embarrassing for both of you."

"When one of the bank tellers had come to talk to me about an issue. I presumed from the extended roundness of her stomach that it had to do with maternity leave, so I started in on the conversation instead of letting her state her concern."

"What happened when she said she wasn't pregnant?"

"I apologized and asked her why she was there."

"Did she accept your apology?"

"At that moment, yes. It happened six years ago when I started at the bank, but to this day, she glares, and I swear she sucks her teeth every time she sees me. I will never make such a detrimental mistake again."

"Good," Precious said with a single nod. "And yes, that was my stomach. I'm hungry. I'm heading to my mother's chop bar for dinner."

He got the sense she might want to invite him out of cordiality, but held back. He didn't blame her. "Can I join you?"

Dark eyes narrowed, and he braced for the impact of her next words.

"Why?"

"Because we seem to be having a good time, and we're both hungry." A simple, direct, honest answer that wouldn't have satisfied him if he'd received it.

Precious crossed her arms over her chest. His vision drifted to her full, perky breasts where her new position showed off the crest of skin slightly lighter than her neck. His gaze lingered for the briefest of seconds before flying up to her face.

"You declined my offer of lunch. What's changed?"

Nothing. She was still Ewe, and he was still his father's child who would never go against the man he respected most in the world, despite his shortcomings. He couldn't let her know. Her own regard for his father would change, and she may decline to work with him. His father liked Precious, and she was improving his mobility. The older man's preference that his children not get involved with someone from the Ewe tribe was longstanding. Ridiculous, in Osei's opinion.

He'd give her his non-offensive answer of why he didn't tend to date. "I have time right now. Or rather, I made time. I'm usually working on Saturdays, but on Blue Leaf Market days, I take the whole day off. The weekend, actually. This allows me to spend time with my family and friends." Before she could disclaim a friendship with him, he rushed on. "And friends in the making."

"Oh."

Was that disappointment or acceptance at his partial explanation? "I thought since we're having a good time, we could continue it at dinner. What do you say?"

"I am hungry. And my mother won't be able to provide me with the amount of attention I desire while she's running her place so, sure. Let's go as friends."

Precious became more intriguing with every moment they spent together, he'd be happy to shower her with every ounce of attention he had in him. Yet, displeasure speared into his heart to have what he needed from her ricocheted back at him. With every moment they spent together, he wanted more. Sharing a meal would have to suffice. "I'll have to make sure not to ignore you for even a second in order to keep you content."

"You're a fast learner," she said with a wink. "Give me a moment. I'll be right back."

Osei went to the small bookcase they'd moved to the corner of the room and pulled out a book at random. The cover had a sticker of the *Accra Reading Club* on it. He'd never heard of the story or the author. He reached for another book and found the same sticker. A quick perusal of the back covers of those in his hand

and a couple more he took from the shelf, and he decided not to join the book club.

He didn't read as much as he wanted, but his genre of choice was non-fiction and occasionally science fiction. None of the fictional stories he held appealed.

"I'm ready."

Precious wore the same dress as earlier, with a handbag slung over her shoulder. She'd added a touch of make-up, and her skin glowed. He bit his tongue to retain the compliment that sat on the tip and tore his gaze away to the bookshelf.

The citrus, floral, and cocoa butter scent he'd come to associate with her enveloped him. With his back to her, he inhaled deeply.

When he faced her again, she stood a couple of feet away. Close enough to reach out and caress her cheek to feel the silkiness of it. Or to close the space and press his lips against hers and see if the same sparks flew with a kiss as they did when their hands touched.

"Here's the book for the meeting next week," she said.

He looked down at her offering and held back a wince. The title was *Friday Black* by Nana Kwame Adjei-Brenyah. A Ghanaian. Between the excitement on her face and the potential of reading a book by a countryman, he'd give the club and their unappealing books a try. If only to be around Precious.

"Consider it a gift," she said. "I'll buy another copy from Georgina this week."

"Thank you. I'll pay for dinner tonight."

She shook her head and laughed. "That's not going to happen, not at my mom's place. She'd take it as a tremendous insult considering you're there with me. Besides, I think now we're even."

He followed her out and waited as she locked the door. "I doubt it. We'll forever be in your debt for helping our father."

"That's what the big paychecks are for. Let's go before my stomach turns inside out seeking food."

He scrunched his nose. "That sounds disgusting."

"Welcome to the world of hanging out with a healthcare worker. Am I driving, or are you?"

"As much as I'd like to relax and be chauffeured, I'll drive this time considering that you—"

She placed a hand against his chest. "That's the last incidence of mentioning anyone owing anyone. Okay?"

His skin scorched at her touch, he reached up and covered her fingers with his as he searched deep into her eyes. The one thing his father's stroke had taught him was that life wasn't guaranteed. Every second should be lived to the fullest because the future couldn't be predicted.

He longed to experience the woman who stood in front of him. To share something he'd remember for the rest of his life. Moving slow enough so she understood his intention, he closed the space between them. When she didn't budge, he continued as her chin tilted upwards and her lids closed.

The first touch felt as if a small lightning bolt had hit him. And then came the sensation of her soft, full lips responding. He dropped the book as he reached around and framed her hips. Her moan enticed him as she grabbed his neck and tilted her head to the side.

He didn't need any further coaxing to open up when her tongue slid against the seam of his lips. Minty freshness hit his taste buds as their tongues engaged. Breathing in her luxurious scent, he dove in as if he wanted her to be the last meal he'd ever have.

His imagination had been on point when he'd envisioned her responsiveness. Her hands caressing his back, his neck, and holding him close so that every part of his body, from his thighs to his chest, revelled in the softness of her curves.

He grabbed her butt to draw her even closer, only to have her push against his shoulders and step out of his embrace.

The air tensed as their gazes held.

Breathing rapidly, Precious smoothed down her hair while touching her lips with the other hand. "We should go."

He wanted to argue otherwise. To coax her to open her door so they could explore some more, but she was right. Attraction wasn't the only thing that made for compatibility. If his father didn't agree with her being in his life, then it would never happen. He needed to remember that the next time he found it impossible to do anything but devour her.

Chapter Ten

Despite the incredible kiss occupying most of her thoughts as they took the short ride, Precious was able to keep up with the conversation Osei had no problem initiating. Only a freak occurrence of an earthquake could've stopped her from allowing their lips to meet. She rubbed them together to savour the tingles that still remained.

She'd wanted to open her door and push him through it so they'd see where things went, but she'd held back. Being busy at work wasn't the only thing that had kept him from accepting her lunch invitation. As her mother always told her in one of the many proverbs she liked to share, *Monkeys play by sizes*.

Just like she'd resisted men from the Ashanti tribe, the same happened with some of them and other tribes when it came to relationships with Ewes. He was smart enough not to directly admit it to be the issue, but she sensed it. Just as she'd been willing to try dating an Ashanti, even after all she'd been through, the one person she wanted seemed to hold her tribe against her.

It hadn't stopped their attraction from flaring, though. No matter how ironic she found the situation to be, or how sad it made her to think about losing him, she'd have to keep in mind that whatever happened, Osei wasn't for keeps.

"I didn't know that Aunty Selorm was your mother," Osei said as he pulled into one of the few parking spaces in front of Eat All Chop Bar.

She gave him a double take. "I wouldn't have figured you ate at chop bars."

"And miss some of the best local dishes? Sha. I dey chop oooo."

She laughed as the pidgin rolled off his tongue. This was the first time he'd spoken anything to her other than proper English.

"I mentioned I attended university," he added. "I can remember only one date I took to a restaurant. All else were chop bars. Affordable and delicious. The combination can't be beat."

"The one you took to a restaurant must've been special."

He shrugged. "I thought so at the time. Until she blew my monthly food budget and never spoke to me again."

They hiked up a small slope into the brightly lit, open-spaced area enclosed by bamboo fencing. Osei chose an empty table and chair combo that seated two.

"To be honest," he said. "With its more sophisticated ambiance, this place is more like a restaurant than the traditional small chop bar that it used to be before she converted it."

Precious looked around attempting to see from his perspective. The atmosphere was clean and simple, with a few potted plants interspersed around the periphery. Fans rotated slowly from the high ceilings, keeping the patrons cool. Waitstaff buzzed around delivering clay bowls filled to the brim with food. The space was crowded with people speaking in their local languages.

She was proud of what her mother had accomplished. "She tried to keep it as unpretentious as she could when she expanded. Her intention was to always be seen as a chop bar. The food is still as delicious, and that's all that counts. What do you want to eat? I'll put our orders in when I go say hello to my mother."

His menu stayed closed on the table. "Fufu with palm nut soup. Goat meat, tilapia, and snail."

"Hmmm. That sounds good, minus the snail." The heavy meal of pounded casava and plantain would probably still be digesting in her stomach at four in the morning, but it would be worth it. "Anything to drink?"

"Star. A small one since I'm driving."

"You can go for a big one, if you want. We could take a walk to clear it out of your system. I'm going to need a stroll after such a large dinner."

"Then make it a boss."

"Will do. I'll be right back."

She felt the heat of his gaze as she walked away. The slight turn she made to greet one of the employees proved her correct, and she put a little more swing in her hips. A quick stop at the bar to ask for two beers to be delivered to her table, and she was in the back where all the action happened.

The cooking area was where her mother had started and was always where someone could find her. This evening, she used her muscles and a sturdy wooden spoon to stir corn and casava dough in a huge pot over a gas fire to make banku. When she saw Precious, she handed the task to a nearby worker.

"My daughter," she said in Ewe. "It's good to see you. Are you here to work? We are fully staffed."

Once a week, Precious came to help her mother out if needed. The woman had raised her when she didn't have to, so she tried to do her small part to help the success of her business.

"Hi, Mama. Not tonight. I brought a friend to eat," she replied in her mother's language.

"What should I serve?"

She repeated the two orders. "I'll take them out."

"Go and be with your friend."

Precious went back to their table. Osei's phone lit up his face, but as soon as she sat, he put it away. The gesture impressed her when she wished it didn't matter.

"The food is on its way."

"Another benefit of a chop bar. Fast service."

"True."

He raised his bottle. "A toast to my father's renewed health, good food, and a new friendship."

Dissatisfied at the last aspect of the toast when she wanted more, she pasted on a smile and clinked his full glass with her bottle. Knowing how obsessed she was about having drinks opened in front of her, Mawuli had left it capped. She took out a bottle opener from her bag, removed the cap, and poured it into the waiting glass before drinking the refreshing beer.

"I asked the guy who delivered the drinks, Mawuli, to open yours, too, but he shook his head and walked away."

He'd learned the server's name? When would he stop impressing her?

"I insist on always watching a container be opened in front of me." Not wanting to lay a depressing blanket over the evening, she kept the reasoning short. "I once had a drug slipped into my drink. Luckily, I was with my friend Lamisi who's like a bodyguard when we go out, and she noticed I was acting weird. She got me into a taxi, and we went home so nothing happened. I don't remember much from that night, but I never leave my drink unattended."

His nostrils flared with what she could only assume to be anger on her behalf. "Humans can be the basest of creatures. I'm glad you were all right."

Her mother showed up carrying a tray with two covered Asankas. She placed two spoons beside the clay bowls on the table before looking up at her guest.

"Osei?"

He got to his feet, and her mother hugged him.

"Aunty Selorm. *Efoa*?"

"*Me fo. Wo ha ɛfoa?*"

"*Me fo.*"

"It has been a long time since you've visited me," her mother said in English after their greet and response moment in Ewe.

"Yes. Work has been keeping me occupied."

Her mother turned accusing eyes towards Precious. "If you had told me your friend was Osei, I would have doubled the portions."

Forcing her eyes to return to their normal size and her jaw to function after witnessing the interaction between the two, Precious shook her head. "I didn't know you knew each other."

"Yes. Osei has been a patron here for many years. When the man did a shoddy job of putting up the bamboo fencing, it was Osei who fixed it."

"That was you?"

"Yes."

"You were overseas studying at the time," her mother said.

He'd won her mother's heart over five years ago. Even longer, since she'd considered him a regular customer before she'd expanded.

"Eat before the food gets cold. I'll return to speak with you soon." She went to the next table and greeted them. Once she was among her patrons, she'd check up on all of her present customers before returning to the kitchen to dominate.

After going to the sink to wash their hands, they dug into their food fingers first. All conversation ceased at that point.

With her bowl still filled with soup, but empty of everything else, Precious leaned against her seat and sighed with the contentment only a full belly could elicit.

Osei spooned up his soup until nothing but drops remained clinging to the sides of the bowl. "I won't stay away for so long again."

She had too many questions, but the food crushing her throat only allowed her to grunt in appreciation.

Her beer sat forgotten as Osei drained the rest of his.

"Where do you put all of that food?"

He raised an arm and flexed. "The gym and woodworking are a metabolic dream."

She wished she could be living that dream. If she were wearing jeans, the fat roll would be escaping over the top. She appreciated her shape, especially the backside of herself, but sometimes, she wished she could show off the six pack of abs she had hidden below a strategically placed layer of fat.

Her mother dragged over a chair. "Where did you meet?"

"I'm working with his father." She kept it brief and confidential. "Did you know Osei makes beautiful furniture?"

"Yes. I told him he should stop the work that causes him so much stress and do what makes him happy."

"The market is saturated with furniture makers and sellers," he said.

"You see, Osei. If there were no elephant in the jungle, the buffalo would be a great animal."

Despite hearing such proverbs throughout her life, most of them were lost on Precious, and this disappointed her mother to no end. Direct and to the point was her motto, and she had no need to sort through words in order to gain an understanding of what was being said.

This didn't seem to be Osei's issue as he nodded in solemn agreement. "Just like you're the mighty chop bar surrounded by many chop bars who don't measure up to you."

The corners of her mother's eyes crinkled with her broad smile. "The same is true for your ability to dominate. There are many furniture makers, but it doesn't mean your work isn't needed. Most importantly that you won't succeed."

Wanting to jump onto the encouragement bandwagon, Precious hauled herself up so her back was straight. "Your items are unique. While I was doing my own exploration at the market, your assistant sold to three different people. If you add an online component with international shipping, you'd be huge."

"Listen to my daughter. She's very smart."

Precious grinned. The pride her mother expressed in her never got old. "*Akpe na wo*," she thanked in the language that relayed her deepest gratitude.

The woman who'd been generous with her time, love, and support got to her feet with a grunt. "Have fun. Precious, I'll see you at the house tomorrow."

It wasn't a request by anyone's stretch of the imagination. "Yes, Mama."

"Have a good night, Osei."

"You, too, Aunty Selorm."

Precious watched as she walked away with a slight hitch in her step. "If anyone told her to stop running this place, they'd find themselves on the wrong side of a coal tar enema."

He winced. "I don't believe there is a right side of that. She loves it."

"It would be good if she took more time to relax, though. I talked her down from working six days a week to four. But she's still here on her supposed days off."

"I hear you, but she should do what makes her happy for as long as she can. It helps her to feel young despite knowing she's growing."

She arched a brow. "You and your wise words."

"My father's, actually. We've been talking a lot more than we ever have. I'm learning so much about him and what he's been through."

She swiped on the condensation sliding down her beer bottle. "That's good to hear. Not everyone gets that opportunity."

"It looks like you have a good relationship with your mother."

"I do. She saved my life." Rather than explain, she got to her feet. "You promised me a walk, and if we don't set off now, I may make my bed on this floor."

He threw his head back with his boisterous laughter. "As clean as this place is, I wouldn't recommend it."

Being with him appeased her spirit and she didn't want this outing with Osei to end. Too bad because it would, and hopefully, she'd release it with grace.

Chapter Eleven

An hour of strolling thought the streets of East Legon was something Osei hadn't done in a very long time. Discussing current events and skirting away from the topic of politics as they enjoyed the cool air and the stars in the sky had been memorable.

At her building, he'd walked her up to her apartment.

"Would you like to come in for some peppermint tea?" Precious asked after she'd unlocked the door. "I find it aids in digestion."

He shouldn't, not after the kiss they'd shared. All night, he'd been tempted to take her in his arms to feel her moulded against him again. The temptation of extending the night with her, even just to talk, won. "I've never had it, but I'll give it a try."

Switching on the light, she paused and took in the room before entering.

"I forgot we'd changed things around. It looks wonderful. It won't take long to get used to. And your stand looks perfect."

His perusal remained more on her as she scoped the room. He hadn't been able to tear his gaze away from her stunning beauty all night.

"It proves you have great taste," he quipped. "Can I please use your restroom?" The beer had made its way through him, and he was bursting to go.

She waved an arm in the direction of the hallway. "The first door on the right."

He entered the space to find a full bath. After using the facility and washing his hands, curiosity overcame him, and he reached to open the mirrored bathroom cabinet above the sink. Not much in there. An extra box of toothpaste and an unopened toothbrush. Floss. Mouthwash. Vicks Vapor rub.

A little dissatisfied, he closed the panel. What was he expecting to find? Something that would make him like her a little less. A sachet of cocaine would've been ideal.

He found her in the kitchen. "Is there anything I can do to help?"

She jumped as if startled before turning to face him. "No. I'm waiting for the water to boil. Do you want sugar in your tea? I usually drink peppermint tea without it."

"What about milk?"

The scrunch of her nose proved more of an answer than her verbal one. "Not in herbal tea. Or would you prefer regular tea? Or coffee? I'll warn you that it's been in the house untouched since I've moved in."

"No thanks to the coffee. I'll try something new. No sugar like yours."

"You can have a seat in the hall, if you'd like. You know where everything is," she said with a grin. "Including the remote for the television."

He rested against the counter and crossed his arms over his chest so he wouldn't reach out and pull her into a hug. "I'll wait here, if you don't mind."

"Not at all."

The silence was comfortable as they shared the space, giving him the courage to explore. "Can I ask you a personal question?"

She mirrored his pose and tilted her head. "Yes, but it doesn't mean I'll answer."

He chuckled. "Fair enough."

The kettle she'd placed on the stove whistled. She moved to turn it off and poured the water into the cups with tea bags in them.

When the water turned green, for a moment, he reconsidered having regular tea.

"Would you like biscuits?"

The only sweet thing he wanted was a taste of her lips again. "No, thank you."

He picked up her new favourite tray which held two teaspoons along with the teas and went to the hall. She placed two of his coasters onto the coffee table before settling the mugs on them. They sat on the couch next to each other, but not close enough to accidentally touch.

"What's your question? You need to know that I don't have much of a temper, but if it's profane, I will kick you out."

"Nothing *that* personal."

"Good."

"Aunty Selorm once mentioned that she was as proud of you as a daughter as your parents would've been. What happened to your parents?"

She closed her eyes for a few seconds. When she opened them, they were sad, but her expression determined. "When I was eight, we all got cholera. They died, and I survived."

His heart plummeted at her loss. "You have my condolences."

"Aunty Selorm, as you so fondly call her, was my mother's best friend. When—" she paused and looked away, focusing on the blank screen of the television for a moment before meeting his gaze. "She took me in. Both of her husbands had died and left her with no children. I was it for her, and she treated me like the child she'd never had. I will always be grateful. She officially adopted me, and I changed my last name to hers."

Precious reached over and removed the tea bags from the mugs. "I think it's cool enough to drink."

He took his cup and blew on the edge of the liquid as he pondered her story. The first sip left a minty taste on his tongue.

"How is it?"

He took another sip. "I could get used to it."

The pleasant sound of her laughter filled the room as she got out of her seat and went to the kitchen. When she returned, she had a pot of sugar and another teaspoon in her hands. "Try it sweet."

After dissolving the sugar, he tasted it again. "This is better."

"Good."

He set the mug down and focused on her. "What happened to your family? Didn't your parents have siblings? Cousins? Parents?"

"All the above, but no one wanted to take me in. If it wasn't for Mama, I would've been out on the streets or sent to an orphanage."

The traumatic pain she'd gone through as a little girl caused his chest to tighten and he lay a hand on her shoulder to console. "I'm sorry to hear that."

"Things worked out well. Look at me. I'm successful and loved. I don't need them."

He heard the slight hitch in her voice and reached down to take her hand. A perfect fit in his as heat wound up his arm. "They've missed out on knowing a wonderful woman."

She blinked up at him. "Thank you."

"I get the sense you may have been a holy terror as a child, though."

"Not even a little bit." She touched her chest. "I was an angel. Too afraid of being kicked out to do anything wrong."

"Aunty Selorm would have always supported you."

Her head ticked to the side. "How do you know?"

His turn to confess. "Because it's what she did with me."

Chapter Twelve

It must've been the comfort of being with Osei, holding his hand, and exposing her past that had made Precious mishear what he'd said. She squared off to face him. "Pardon me?"

"When I was younger, before you came around, my parents lived in the same neighbourhood as your mother's chop bar. Back then, it was a small place, but always packed. I must've been eight or nine at the time, but I was continually getting into mischief with my friends. When your mother noticed, she called us all over and spoke to us. For some reason, I took what she said to heart. I think it was the way she communicated, as if we were matured rather than children."

She listened, her incredulousness rising at their shared history as he stroked a calloused thumb against her knuckles.

"It didn't stop me from getting in trouble," he continued. "But I went out of my way to greet her when I was nearby. One day, she offered me a job. It was only sweeping, but I felt special at being given the responsibility. I worked at her place for two years until my parents moved to Cantonments. I would go back and visit whenever I could, but it wasn't often."

"I don't remember ever seeing you."

He shrugged. "Ships that pass in the night, I guess."

"And here we are," she whispered as she slumped against the couch, taking it all in.

How could they be linked by the same woman and she'd never heard of him? Then again, her mother had helped many children in the area over the years—she'd even sponsored a few to attend school. Oddly enough, her mother had helped to turn Osei's life around, and now, they were fighting their attraction for each other.

The minutes ticked by as she processed and tried to come to grips with everything. So many things might have prevented their meeting. His father could've been taken to any other hospital in Accra. Daniel could've gone against his greedy nature and declined the more lucrative job. Daniel could've asked another colleague to take the assignment. So many hindrances she could come up with, but none of them had materialized.

Viewing it all from another angle, she accepted that they'd have encountered each other at some point, perhaps at the Blue Leaf Market. He, like his handicrafts, certainly would've caught her eye. The words fate and destiny kept repeating in her brain, and she liked them being there.

She'd never been someone to pretend something wasn't what it was, so she pushed herself up to a full sitting position to face him. "What are we doing, Osei? Friends don't kiss like we did and hold hands. Am I right to say that you're attracted to me?"

"Yes."

"So, what's going on?" She released his hand. "Am I part of your free monthly weekend?"

His head jerked back, giving him a slight double chin as his brows drew together. "No. I like being with you. And we have chemistry, but I'm not ready for a relationship."

He wasn't a young boy anymore either.

"Are you seeing someone?" She held up a hand before he could speak. "Wait. Let me guess. You're engaged to a Ghanaian who lives in the US, and you'll fly off once she sets you up with papers."

The unexpectedness of his guffaw caused her to stare.

"Do you watch a lot of movies?" he asked.

She shrank back a little. "No, but I have friends who talk about their experiences. These things happen. One day, they're dating someone they think will marry them, and the next, the man is flying to another country after the woman abroad comes for an extravagant wedding before escaping Ghana."

"I'm not seeing anyone right now. In Ghana or anywhere else in the world. Second, I have no intention of ever leaving Ghana. My family is here. I live a good life, and I'm happy."

Another thing they had in common. Drawn off the topic she should've sunk her teeth into, she nodded. "Me, too. I was homesick when I was in the UK. Ghana is good, and I learned to appreciate it more when I was away."

"Did people wonder why you returned instead of staying abroad?"

"They still do when they discover where I got my master's degree. Sometimes, I want to tell them to leave the country if they think it's so great out there."

"I've travelled to the US for a conference and loved the experience, but knew it wouldn't be where I'd want to settle down. My heart is in Ghana and always will be."

A swirl of warmth filled her chest as she looked into his eyes, wishing she were in his heart as well.

No. You will not *be distracted by an agreement on a topic.*

"I'm not dating anyone either," she admitted.

"I figured as much," he said with an arrogance that reminded her of when they first met.

She saw him as a blur through squinted eyes.

Holding up both hands, he pushed back into the couch. "I engage with and read people for a living. I can tell when someone is honest and when they're shady. You're in the honest category."

The argumentative tension eased out of her, and she relaxed her spine. "You're right. I can't stand liars, so I don't do it myself."

"I like that about you. Along with other things I've discovered. We'd make a good match."

She tamped down the giddiness bubbling up. "I hear the *but* you aren't saying."

Osei pinched his fingers over the bridge of his nose and sighed before letting his hand fall to his lap. "Right now, I don't have the time to commit to anyone."

An idea hit her with the force of a strong alcoholic drink, and she sat up straight. He had just presented the perfect situation. She only had it in her to date someone for a few months before she got bored with him. By the time she got around to letting her partner know, the guy was sprung on her and things got messy. That didn't have to happen with Osei. They could explore their attraction without thinking they had to change their social media relationship status.

The more she thought about it, the better it sounded. She had nothing to lose with her proposal. The worst he could say was no. And possibly call her a slut for being open about her sexuality, but she couldn't see that happening.

"Precious?"

The concern in his voice brought her out of her ruminations. "Yes?"

"Are you okay?"

Never better.

"I had an idea." She took a sip of her lukewarm tea. "What if we kept things physical?"

His features transformed into an expression she couldn't decipher.

Since she'd opened the can, she may as well dive in. "You know the expression friends with benefits? That would be us."

"No feelings," he finally said.

Taking the opportunity to be a little saucy, she scraped a short nail against his bicep. "There would be lots of feeling. Just no emotions."

His Adam's apple bobbed. "As long as we're both clear this is a temporary situation, and we can back out at any time. And it stays between us."

Raising a hand as if taking an oath, she hid her excitement at the prospect of a sexual relationship with a solemn nod. "Yes, to all of the above. We have to be safe, too. Condoms at all times. Every time."

His gaze became hooded as he stared at her lips. "Every single time."

Her core throbbed at the passion in his voice. He leaned forward, looking intent on kissing her when she remembered what they'd just promised. She jumped to her feet to avoid a kiss that would lead to a whole lot more. "I don't have condoms."

He sucked in air through his teeth as if splashed with cold water. "Me neither."

Precious used the arm of the chair as a barrier as her libido cooled. Odd how neither of them mentioned finding an open petrol station to buy some. Maybe they weren't ready yet. Her body was, but she needed more time to adjust to the thought of it. Get to know him a little better.

"We still have the friends part." He patted the cushion next to him. "Come and relax. We'll start things slow."

Precious took her time returning to her seat.

"You can get a little closer."

When she shifted so the heat of his body seeped into her, he placed an arm around her and pulled her in closer. She rested her head against his shoulder.

"Tell me, Precious. Do you or have you ever played any sports?"

She melted into him as her muscles released the last bit of tension. She'd get the chance to squelch this attraction while thoroughly enjoying his company. It would be a win-win.

Chapter Thirteen

"Chale," Osei said to his best friend Enoch as they clasped hands and came in for a hug that ended with light pounding on the back. "It's been too long."

"Chale," Enoch responded with the local Ghanaian version of dude. "My eyes are playing tricks on me this day." He looked behind him and tapped his wife on the shoulder. "Am I imagining him, or is he real?"

Freda, a petite woman nearly half her husband's size, also came with a grand personality.

"If you are, then we are both losing it." She jumped up and hugged Osei. "Allah has answered my prayers today. You don't know how much time I spent at the mosque when I sent the invitation to you. Weeks and weeks of hoping you would attend. And here you are. My prayers are powerful, oooo."

Osei laughed at the woman he'd gotten along with the moment Enoch had introduced her to him six years ago. "Yes, they are. Just as powerful as you are dramatic, considering you just had the baby seven days ago, and Enoch called to invite me here. How are you, Freda?"

"I'm better now that I've seen you." She placed a hand on Enoch's arm. "Spend time with your elusive friend before he disappears, never to be seen until our next outdooring."

"Please tell me the baby's name before anyone else. Does it start with an O and end with an i, by any chance?" he teased. The naming ceremony would reveal to the world what they'd be calling their week-old baby.

Freda slapped his shoulder. "You!" And then, she laughed as she walked away.

Enoch's expression became serious. "Thank you for coming."

"Chale, you're a father now. Congratulations! I don't care how busy I am, I wouldn't miss your first child's outdooring."

"I'm sure it helps that we held it at six in the morning before work started. Otherwise, you wouldn't have come."

He should've been wounded, but facts were facts. "I still can't believe the same man who filled our bathtub with ice back in college and packed beer into it so we could party all Easter weekend long in Kwahu is a father. How's it going?"

The joy in Enoch's smile said it all. "It's exhausting. I have never been so afraid of messing up another person's life, but I love it. Wait until you see my boy. He's perfect. Except when he's crying his lungs out in the middle of the night." He hit his chest with both hands. "I'm glad his food doesn't come from me."

Osei laughed. "We need to make time to hang out."

"Huh. Not me, ooo. You."

Guilt assuaged him as he remembered the instances he'd cancelled with his friends to take care of work issues. "I'm changing. Learning how to dedicate more time to relaxing."

A large hand crashed against his shoulder. "I'll believe it when I see it. Or maybe when you quit Allegiant Bank. You weren't like this at your last place."

Osei shrugged. "With more money comes more responsibilities."

"Not at the expense of enjoying life. You used to be good at that."

Freda, carrying their child, caught Enoch's eye and waved him over.

"We're about to start," Enoch announced before going to his family.

Why was everyone encouraging him to leave his job? Yes, it took up all his time. Stressed him out consistently and left him with no social life, but they compensated him well to do work he'd like if he weren't performing two people's duties. It wasn't that he needed a new job, but to have his boss fired so he could get credit for his input.

During the short ceremony, two things kept hammering away at him. Precious and how he hadn't seen her in six days took up most of the space. Not like he was avoiding her—they texted and spoke every day, but he hadn't made an effort to see her since she'd made her proposition.

The moment had been sexy as hell, and he'd kicked himself twelve times over for not being prepared or offering to go out and buy condoms. He'd wanted her, constantly wanted her, but it hadn't felt right at that moment. Yet, he didn't regret the time they'd spent together. They'd fallen asleep on her couch after talking and laughing. It had been the most relaxing time he'd had with a woman that he could recall. The only kiss they'd shared had been a chaste one he'd given her on the cheek when he'd left at two in the morning.

As amazing as the proposal had been, he still couldn't believe how wonderfully bold she'd been to bring it up. He wasn't sure he could honour the part about keeping his emotions out of whatever stirred between them. How could he when she was intelligent, generous, kind, confident, beautiful, and so amazing she stayed on his mind?

And best of all, she'd admitted to wanting him as much as he did her. How would he not fall for her? He loved a woman who knew what she wanted and how to get it. Not love. No, that would be stupid, premature, and foolish. Yet, with every opportunity he spent with her, with every text and conversation they exchanged, he liked her even more.

That's why he'd had to stay away from her for the week. He'd intentionally left his home long before she'd arrive and returned after he knew she'd be done with the evening session with his father. Avoidance, when you wanted to see someone, proved exhausting.

Osei left the outdooring wondering when his life had gotten so twisted. He wanted simplicity back, and he knew what he had to do to get it. Break things off with Precious before they even started so he didn't have to worry about either of them getting hurt when he had to cut things off with her later anyway. She wasn't the woman he'd end up with. Not if he wanted peace in his family.

***

Precious had half-expected vicious knocking at her door last Sunday, with Osei standing on the other side carrying an industrial sized box of condoms. She'd gone to the first open pharmacy she could find after church and purchased her own multipack. The irony hadn't been lost on her, but she didn't care.

It didn't happen. A week without sex when she'd expected some had left her irritated and the batteries in her vibrator drained. It should've been Osei she'd worn out.

Maybe he'd been telling the complete truth about why he refused to date her. She couldn't be with a guy who refused to prioritize her over his job. Text messages and sparse phone conversations wouldn't be enough. Now that she completely understood who she was dealing with, she could proceed to move on with her life. Without Osei as her friend or the bulging benefit that had pressed into her during their one and only make out session.

Sitting in the office of the latest bank she'd placed a loan application with, she expected to hear positive news. After being rejected by four other banks, she'd worked on her proposal with the help of an investment banker friend and had handed in a flawless business plan they couldn't pass up. Her rehabilitation centre was a money maker waiting to happen, and she was just the person to open it. She had the experience and the drive. The only thing she lacked? The cash.

The nameplate on the banker's desk read Anita Cudjoe. She was hoping to link good news with the name.

Anita looked away from her computer and linked her hands on her desk. "Thank you for applying for a loan with Coastal Development Bank, Ms. Kpodo. I'm sorry, but unfortunately, at this time, we can't offer you the loan."

Stumped at the unexpected news, it took a moment for Precious to collect her thoughts. Wailing, "But whyyyyy!" wouldn't be professional. "Can you please give me the reasons?"

"In this current economic market, the bank has become stringent with its lending criteria. We acknowledge the rehabilitation centre as unique, but you will be starting from the ground up as a sole first-time business owner at the helm with very little collateral."

The woman had looked Precious in the eyes as she'd given her speech. The refusal wasn't personal, but it felt like it as her throat tightened. Needing to get out of there before the burning behind her eyes turned into tears, she stood and offered a hand to Anita. "Thank you for your consideration."

"I wish you the best of luck, Ms. Kpodo."

"Thank you." Precious replied before doing an about face with the precision of a soldier on parade. Her stride was brisk as she walked through the lobby of the air-conditioned bank into the afternoon dry, hot Harmattan air. Holding it together became harder as she got into her car and drove down the street heading towards Cantonments.

She'd be early for her appointment with Mr Aboagye, but as soon as she got to the first traffic light, her vision started to blur. She pulled over when she got the opportunity and let the tears drench her face and shirt as she searched frantically for the handkerchief in her bag. She gave up and sniffled the mucous threatening to run out of her nose. Crossing her arms on the steering wheel, she rested her head against her forearms.

The silent tears turned into shoulder-shaking sobs.

She deserved to have her dreams come to fruition. Why wasn't it happening? What was she doing wrong? The pain dug deep into her, and she bawled.

The thoughts of being a failure transitioned into missing her parents and wondering why they'd had to leave her. Why her family had not claimed her all those years ago and had never reached out for her. Those tumbled into the emptiness of her romantic life which inevitably brought thoughts of Osei and how he'd avoided her for a week knowing she'd be in his home.

The tears refused to abate as the negative thoughts fuelled them. Would she ever find love? He wasn't the one for her, but she wished he was. Which all looped back around to why it was impossible for her to get what she desired out of life.

The tears eventually stopped, and the hiccups started. Avoiding the mirror, she reached her hand into her bag to make one last attempt at finding the handkerchief. She found it and wiped her face.

Daring to look at herself in the rear-view mirror, she cringed. Her eyes would get puffier even if she didn't go into another crying fit, which would happen the moment anyone showed concern. Someone in the Aboagye family would ask what was wrong, and she'd never be able to face them again if she broke down in front of them.

Grabbing her phone, she called Mr Aboagye.

"Hello, Precious."

She released a weak smile at the clarity of his voice and the enthusiasm. He'd been improving with every session. She wished she could bottle his motivation and energy.

"I'm sorry, Mr Aboagye, but I won't be able to make the session this evening." She wiped her nose with the handkerchief.

"Are you okay? You sound hoarse."

She sniffled and bit her quivering lower lip. "I'm fine, but I need to deal with an urgent issue that just came up."

For once, she'd put herself first. The ice cream she'd stop to purchase, and an encouraging talk with Lamisi, would help with the healing.

"Sure," he said with a note of hesitance. "As long as you're okay. Will I see you tomorrow morning?"

Only if she didn't look like she'd gotten punched in the eyes by a professional boxer. A treatment of cold cucumbers would bring down the swelling, though. "Yes. I'll be there at the same time."

"Good. I'll work on the exercises you taught me. You take care of yourself."

"Thank you."

Hauling in a shuddering breath when she ended the call, she thrust her shoulders back. Despite taking this bank loan denial harder than the others, it wouldn't be the end. She'd just have to figure out another way to make her dream come true. One day, she'd be the proud owner of a rehabilitation centre people would clamour to.

That day was turning out to be a little later than she'd initially planned.

Chapter Fourteen

In the two weeks Precious had been working with his father, she'd never cancelled. Twice a week during the work week, and once on Saturday morning for an extended session as per his father's wish. The consistency his dad had been putting into the sessions was paying off. Osei only had to supervise as his father transferred himself out of the bed and onto the bathroom chair. He no longer needed to assist him to have a bath. The strength in his left side had improved considerably, and if things kept going the way they were, his father would be walking independently very soon.

Last night when his father had mentioned Precious hadn't been able to make their session, Osei had become worried enough to call her. When there'd been no answer, he'd sent her a text message asking if she was okay. Her reply had been short, stating she was fine and had a personal issue to deal with.

What more could he say except to hope things went her way? Showing up at her apartment would be out of order considering they were only getting to know each other, the process made even slower with him backing away.

That's why instead of leaving the house before her arrival as had been his early morning routine of being a coward and avoiding her, he'd waited. He'd see her at the book club meeting at two, but he couldn't wait that long to make sure she was okay. His conscience wanted to verify it wasn't because of him she'd had to take a personal day off. Not that Precious seemed to be a clingy sort of woman, but she'd put herself out there. Twice. And he hadn't jumped at the chance to spend time with her like he'd wanted.

Dressed for work in a casual pair of khakis and a short-sleeved shirt because it was technically his day off, he waited in the hall with his father. They watched the morning news, discussing the pertinent issues presented. When the doorbell rang, he jumped out of his seat. "I'll get it."

His father looked at him with greyed brows crinkled together, but said nothing about his jittery behaviour.

When he opened the small gate, his heart hurt to see Precious' eyes slightly puffy and red. He squelched the need to gather her into his arms and hold her until the pain she'd experienced dissolved. He stepped out and closed the metal. "What's wrong?"

She shook her head and gave him an unconvincing smile. "I'm fine."

Her voice sounded a little gravely.

He reached out to cup her face, but let his hand fall when she stepped out of reach. He ignored the sting it caused. "You've been crying."

Moving forward as if she could pass through him, she waved a hand. "It's okay. I'd like to get inside. I feel badly about missing my appointment with your father yesterday."

He stepped to the side to completely block her path. Having seen that she'd been upset enough to still present the remnants of her pain, he needed to know what had caused it so he could solve the problem. "You can tell me what happened. I might be able to help."

The curl of her upper lip into a snarl signalled he'd made a major mistake.

"This doesn't concern you. Now move out of my way."

Digging deep to put his personal feelings aside, he gathered his HR persona in order to gain her trust. He rotated so they stood at ninety-degree angles and she had complete access to the gate.

"You're absolutely right, and I'm sorry. I was concerned because you're consistent when it comes to working with my father." He waited a beat. "Please go inside. He's looking forward to the session. I'll see you at the book club meeting this afternoon."

She whipped her head towards him. "Are you still attending?"

"I didn't read the book for nothing."

Her eyes sparkled. "Did you enjoy it?"

Not even in the slightest. The writing was good, a couple of the short stories had captured his interest, and he was happy to support a Ghanaian writer, but magical realism wasn't anywhere near his preferred genre. He kept his expression neutral. "You'll have to wait until the book club meeting."

She pressed her lips together. "I was thinking of skipping it, but now, I need to go."

This time, his hand made contact with her shoulder without her flinching, and he squeezed. "I look forward to hearing what you thought about it."

"Good." Her gaze went to the gate, and as if she'd made a decision, returned to his eyes. "Since we'll be going to the same place, would you mind giving me a ride? I've been trying to be more conscious about the environment and petrol."

He bounced on his toes as the heaviness between them cleared. "No problem."

Her smile seemed genuine.

"Since the venue is closer to my place, how about meeting me there?" She dipped her head. "At about one-thirty?"

"Sounds like a plan."

Their eyes clung for a several seconds as he resisted leaning over to kiss her. He'd missed the fullness of her mouth responding to him, her body pliant and yielding against his. It had taken a massive amount of discipline to stay away from her during the week.

The recognition of his stupidity hit him hard. They could've been enjoying each other. She might have easily confided in him if he'd been around. Been a friend as he said he'd be.

When she broke eye contact and went through the gate, he followed. He got the sense that despite fighting himself and the reasons for staying away, he'd always prefer to be with her, which didn't scare him as much as it once would've.

***

"Yes, I'm okay." Precious sprayed perfume onto the base of her neck. "You really helped talk me down last night. I'm sorry I bit into your time with Blaise."

"He understood," Lamisi said. "Besides, it was my turn to pick a show, and I chose a documentary, *Dancing with the Birds*. He shooed me away as soon as he heard you needed me and then proceeded to watch one of the furiously fast films."

Precious chuckled, but didn't correct her friend. "I did a lot of thinking last night after going over the five banks' feedback. They can't all be wrong, so I've decided to hold off on my plans to open the rehab centre. Things just don't seem to be coming together for me right now, but at least, I have a good job that I love."

"Are you sure?" Lamisi asked. "There are still some banks you haven't tried yet."

The decision she'd made still caused her heart to tighten when she thought of it. Her dream. Her baby. Delayed for who knew how long? But she wasn't giving up, merely taking a detour. "Yes. I'm not jumping up and down with joy about it, but I know it's the right decision. I have years to get the rehab centre off the ground. In the meantime, I'll work on networking to get potential backers. Maybe find a therapist partner to split the business with?"

"As long as you're okay with the decision, I support you."

Her friend was her number one cheerleader. "Or I could land a billionaire sugar daddy who would set me up."

Lamisi sucked her teeth. "As if you'd exploit anyone."

She was right. Precious didn't have it in her. Her mother would've been more than willing to help sponsor her, but she couldn't bring herself to ask. Not when her mom had been so generous in assisting her to go abroad for her master's. The scholarship she'd received from the university hadn't covered living expenses. Her savings could've only gotten her so far even when she'd planned to get a part-time job to supplement, so her mother had once again saved her.

"You're right." She sighed in the most dramatic way she could. "Being honest is such a burden sometimes. Wouldn't it be great if we could use and abuse people?"

"Just for fun," Lamisi added.

"Neither of us could get away with it. We're too good."

"Speak for yourself, Precious. I'm the wife of a hiplife artist now. I can be bad to the bone."

They laughed at the ridiculousness of the comment. Blaise Ayoma was one of the most wholesome hiplife artists in Ghana. He'd made a promise to his parents he'd been successful in keeping.

"I have to go. Osei is coming to pick me up for the book club meeting."

"Osei." Lamisi stretched out the name. "As of last night, he was persona non grata because he had yet to come over and…how did you put it? Take you up on your offer. Which I can't believe you made."

"Well, believe it." She'd never make that mistake again. And still, she'd asked him to drive her to the meeting. When it came to Osei, invitations flew out of her mouth before her brain could rein them in.

"Are you sure nothing can happen with him?"

She nodded. "Yes. We may be attracted to each other, but no matter how much I try to let go of it, I still have a deep-rooted fear of the whole Ashanti/Ewe dynamic."

"Which is understandable considering what you've been through, but can you please do me one favour?"

"Keep an open mind?" Precious mocked what she knew would be her friend's advice.

"When did you become psychic?" Lamisi asked with a chuckle. "You took the words straight from my head."

"It's not as if I haven't known you for donkey years."

"Seriously, though. Please take my wisdom to heart. You never know if Osei might be your husband to be."

"As happy as I'd love to be with my man one day, I doubt Osei is the one."

"Why? You like him, right?"

Too much, but she wouldn't admit it out loud. "I—" Her doorbell rang. "He's here, Lamisi. I've got to go."

"Keep my words in mind and have fun."

"Thanks. Enjoy marking your papers."

"You're hilarious," Lamisi said before hanging up.

With one last look in the mirror, Precious grinned as she assessed the box braids cascading down to the middle of her back. She'd needed a pick-me-up, and getting her hair styled after the session with Mr Aboagye had done the trick. She looked and felt a whole lot better than she had yesterday.

Lamisi's advice kept up a steady drumming in her head as she left her apartment. She only wished she could let go of her past in order to give him a real chance. *If* he wanted one.

Chapter Fifteen

"I'm still shocked you didn't like the book." Precious waited until he'd entered her apartment before closing the door.

"It had its merits, but it wasn't for me. The book club, on the other hand, was enjoyable. Georgina should look into becoming a stand-up comedian because she's hilarious."

"She makes the encounter fun. Would you like some water?"

"No, thank you." He patted his flat stomach as he sat onto the couch. "I never knew sandwiches could be so filling."

"Trying new foods is the fourth perk of the book club," she said as she joined him.

"I get that reading new books is the first. Making friends is the second. What's the third?"

"Laughing and forgetting about the problems of life as you engross yourself in fictional issues, even if it's just for a couple of hours."

She'd peeped him having a good time during the small group discussions they'd been assigned to. Toyin had seen her spying and had winked at her.

"You seem happier than you did this morning." He reached for one of her braids and let it slip through her fingers. "New look, new outlook?"

Ignoring the shiver that raced down her spine, she raised a brow. "Is that how the saying goes?"

"I didn't know there was a saying. I just like seeing you happy."

His words had the ability to melt her heart like butter on freshly baked tea bread. In the morning, she'd been angry with him for ignoring her all week and then having the nerve to get in her face pretending to care about how she felt. When he'd said he was still going to the book club meeting, she'd realized her expectations had been set too high. She'd broken her own rule and added emotions into the mix. Now, she realized her mistake, and the only way to survive being with him was to accept him as someone who wanted to avoid any kind of romantic entanglement. Since she still wanted him in her bed, she'd convinced herself to accept it.

"I'm doing better. Thanks for the ride today. It's relaxing to lounge in the passenger's seat watching all the interesting things that happen in Accra."

"I agree," he admitted. "Next time, you drive."

"So, you'll be reading the next book once Georgina chooses it? I must warn you, she likes to think we're voting for the books she nominates, but she ultimately chooses the one she wants us to read."

"She's a book dictator, then."

"Basically," Precious said with a giggle, wondering how Georgina would view the term. "But she has wonderful intuition."

He grunted. "Not if you consider the one we just read."

"There's no accounting for everyone's taste."

Her stomach flipped when his gaze dropped to her lips and held steady.

"Precious?"

The whisper of her name sent tingles spiralling down her spine. "Yes?"

"Can I kiss you?"

As an answer, she slammed herself into him and plastered her lips against his. Releasing the pressure, she let her mouth glide against his and groaned at his immediate response of gently nipping her lower lip. And then, his tongue brushed against hers in the most delectable way. In. Out. Around. Retreating so that she chased and laved at the sweet heat of his mouth.

Angling her head, she opened to him, and the passion flared. She'd missed this. Had missed him even more.

He lifted and positioned her so she straddled him. Her trousers were no barrier to his hard bulge when she lowered herself and let out a whimper. He kissed her with an intensity that mimicked how her hips rotated against him. She needed more contact than the protective clothing could provide. Being held by a man had never felt so good. Right. Incredible.

Releasing her mouth, he brushed his lips along her jaw and down to her neck, where he found a spot to suck that made her grab onto his shoulders so she wouldn't fall backwards.

"Precious," he rasped out. "You taste as sweet as you smell."

She'd say the same about him if she could formulate anything other than the whimper she let out as he licked the hollow at the base of her neck. His journey south had her arching her back. Raising her shirt, he exposed the yellow lace bra she'd only hoped he'd get the chance to see. The moment she'd seen him at her door, she'd known that what brewed between them wasn't over. She just wouldn't be the one to instigate.

He pushed the cups to the side, and her breasts spilled out.

Osei looked up at her, eyes black with desire as his thumbs rubbed against her peaked nipples. "Perfect."

He licked around the lighter areola and then directly on the dark nipple before blowing on it.

The sensation went straight to her core, and she was sure her wetness would leak through her trousers at any minute. Allowing him to maintain control, she watched as he took the nipple in his mouth and sucked.

"Osei," she moaned as she clung to his shoulders.

He moved to the other breast, causing a flurry of pleasure just as intense.

"I have condoms in my room." Her voice came out husky and low.

"Or should we use the one in my wallet?" he said with his mouth full of her, his hands gripping her ass and kneading.

She raised his head and looked him in the eyes as she ground against him. "There's no need to limit ourselves."

With a groan, he stood them up. Her legs wobbled when her feet touched the floor. Osei removed her top and threw it onto the armchair. Once unhooked, the bra hit the floor. Not to be underdressed, she tugged at his cotton print shirt. He raised his arms and helped her take it off. The singlet went sailing into the air next.

Precious traced her fingers against muscular pecs dusted with curly hair. She strolled around him as her hands felt every ridge and dip along his shoulders and broad back. As she pressed the front of her body against him, his heat seeped into her bare skin as she reached around his hips for the button of his trousers. The zipper was hard to manipulate because of the stiffness beneath, but she was determined. When she'd succeeded, she pushed down his trousers until he could step out of them. She reached into the rim of his boxers, lowering the front to meet his hardness.

His gasp expanded his chest as her fingers circled him. Needing to see what she held, she changed her position so she stood in front of him.

"Uhhhh," was all that came out as she took her first look at the stunning man. When she reached out for him again, he moved just beyond arm's length and pulled up the band to cover himself.

"With the way you're staring at me, I don't know how long I'll last if you touch me again."

Mouth watering, she glanced up into his eyes and licked her lips, wanting to do more than touch. When she went for him, he caught her hands, brought them up to his mouth, and pressed his lips to the inside of her wrist while his tongue circled the sensitive flesh.

She hadn't forgotten her objective, but it felt too good to not enjoy. Romantic and sensual at the same time. While her stomach flipped, her core throbbed, and her skin tingled, he went to work on getting her out of her trousers, followed by her yellow lace panties.

The air cooled her skin as she stood naked in front of him.

His gaze roamed over her body from head to polished toes. "You're glorious."

A bit embarrassed about being completely exposed in the light of day as he assessed her, she fought from flipping her braids over her breasts. "Actually, I'm Precious," she quipped in an attempt to distract him from staring.

His nod coincided with his roving eyes.

"That, too." He pointed towards her newest piece of furniture. "Put your leg up on the second shelf."

"But—"

He removed the plant and placed it on the floor. "Leg up. Now."

She'd have to contemplate just how much and why she liked this domineering side of him. Later. As soon as her foot hit the ledge, he was on his knees. His fingers separated her lower lips, and when his tongue grazed along her clit, her eyes rolled back into her head. Tilting her hips forward, she held onto his broad shoulders to keep her balance. She moaned when he closed his lips around her. Suckling, long licks, and his tongue teasing the bundle of nerves had her whimpering as she held his head in place and moved her hips to his rhythm.

His expert mouth brought her closer to the building climax.

"Oh, my... Oh, my God. Osei," she screeched as her core contracted hard and the orgasm blew her away, making her knees weak. In the background of her pulsating bliss, she felt his large hands holding her so she wouldn't fall.

He got to his feet, and she collapsed into his arms as she shuddered with the impact. She had no words as her heavy breathing took over, and she squeezed her thighs together to draw out the spasms.

Osei walked her to the end of the couch. "Sit here."

As if she could move anywhere on her own, still reeling from what had to be the best orgasm of her life. Osei removed a condom from his wallet and pulled down his boxer briefs. Seeing him again, engorged, her desire to do to him what he'd just gifted her with grew, and she went to her knees.

He shifted away. "What did I tell you to do?"

Her gaze went from his penis to her couch. She went back to the edge, where she perched just her behind so that the material wouldn't get wet from her moisture.

She focused on Osei putting on the condom, wishing her mouth had swapped places with it. When he finished, she was desperate for him to lay her onto the couch, open her wide, and slide into her. She vowed not to presume what went on in his mind when he strode to her and held out a hand.

Placing hers in his, she stood. They took a short walk to the back of the couch.

"Spread your legs."

When she did, she was rewarded with his hand sliding over her belly and between her thighs.

"Yes," she whispered when his fingers slid inside of her before he pulled out and repeated the motion.

He pushed her braids to the side and kissed the back of her neck. "I thought I might have sucked you dry. It's good to know you're still hot and wet for me."

She bent forward and opened her legs wider as she pushed her hips back against him in an open invitation.

"I need more," she panted as he circled the area that his mouth had strummed so perfectly.

His length rested at the juncture of her thighs. Osei was still as a boulder as she rubbed against him, attempting to get him to enter and failing.

"Look at the television screen."

Raising her head, she peered at her flat screen. The image of them wasn't as clear as when looking into a mirror, but her hair flowed down, covering one breast while the other lay exposed as he stood bare-chested behind her.

Osei rubbed her back with one hand and pinched a nipple with another. She gasped at the erotic sight as her core throbbed in response.

He slid his hand down and over her ass before reaching between them. He skimmed his tip against her opening, then along her again, teasing the area already on fire. "I wish you could see us like I can right now. You are so sexy."

"Osei, please. You know what I need." She wiggled her behind against him as she got on her toes and leaned forward. "Give it to me."

That's all it took for him to inch his way into her as she watched them in the flat screen until he filled her completely.

He pulled out slowly and pressed back in. The next time he left her feeling empty, she pushed back hard against him, her breasts jiggling with the impact. "Yes."

From there, their skin slapped with each thrust, Precious becoming wild when he grabbed her hips and lifted her, taking full control as she hung on to the sofa.

"Sweetheart, touch yourself and come with me."

She reached down and rubbed her fingers against her clit as she watched them in the flatscreen. Despite not being able to see them joining like he could, viewing his upper body and face as he thrust into her was the most magnificent thing she'd ever experienced. His presence was everything, and she wondered how she'd gone so long without feeling this deep-souled connection. "Osei, I'm coming."

He stroked harder into her as she climaxed around him. A few thrusts later and he growled as he stiffened behind her.

Their heavy breathing filled the room as reality returned.

"I'm getting rid of the flatscreen and putting up a mirror. One of yours. The biggest you can create."

His chuckle vibrated into her back as he kissed her shoulder. They stayed watching each other for a few seconds longer before he pulled out.

She held back a sigh knowing this was when he'd go clean up, get dressed, and leave because he'd gotten what he'd wanted. Well, so had she. Beyond what she'd expected.

"Let's get cleaned up and then go out to eat. I'm suddenly ravenous."

It wasn't sex he'd been after—he still wanted her company. Excited to have underestimated him, she placed a hand behind his head and drew him down for a kiss that was sweet, but ignited more than hunger for food in her.

He ended it with a peck to her cheek. "Mmmm. Maybe we should stay in. Do you have any food, or should we order?"

"Sounds like a great plan. I hope you like jollof rice and gizzard stew."

"If you, the daughter of Aunty Selorm made it, then I'm sure I'll love it."

She looked up at him. "And about those orders you gave me earlier."

He froze, so she took the opportunity to pinch his muscular ass.

"I liked it. I'm not looking for a dom/sub situation, but damn you were good at telling me what to do."

"Noted."

They went to the bathroom where they bathed together. She ended up tracking the floor with water as she ran for one of the condoms in her bedside drawer when things started to get heated again.

This will be a very beneficial friendship, she thought as he held her against the tile wall and filled her.

Chapter Sixteen

The only reason Osei had left Precious last night was to fulfil his commitment to his father. Monday brought with it a new week and responsibilities he needed to prepare for. Although his father didn't require as much help as when he'd come home six weeks ago, Osei would assist every morning until the man was completely independent. It favoured him, too, because he'd gotten the chance to grow closer to his father.

It had been two weeks since he and Precious had gotten together, and he was hooked. They spoke every night, and there'd been four days where he'd left work at close to normal working hours and ended up at her place where they'd let those benefits overtake the friendship he'd promised. Keeping her satisfied had become a priority.

"I know that smile," his father said after he'd transferred himself into his chair without needing support. "Who is she?"

Osei wiped the grin away and went ahead to deny Precious with the agility of Peter in the Bible. "What? There's no one in my life."

One.

"Come on, son. I know you. I'm not like your mother. You can tell me if you're having something casual. We men have to stick together. Maybe I can give you some advice. If she's anything like your mother, don't let her get away."

Precious possessed many qualities of his mother. They were both beautiful women, inside and out. Worked hard. Laughed frequently. And held their emotions close to their chest. He knew for a fact Precious liked him, but that was all. She shared nothing but her passion with him. He still didn't know what had upset her the one time she'd been crying.

"When the special woman finally does come around, I'll keep your advice in mind, Dada." Denial number two. He had to leave before he was pushed to a third and a cock crowed. "Should I get you anything before I go to work?"

"I'm fine, son. Precious will be here soon."

Osei's muscles flexed as he became overprotective of her even when she wasn't around. Although he hadn't done so in over a month, at least not in his presence, the occasional snide comments his father would make about the Ewes would no longer go unanswered. He didn't know where his father's bias stemmed from, but the mild "oh, Dada," chastisement Osei used to dole out would change. He'd tell his father directly that his tribalistic comments were wrong and would no longer be tolerated.

The older man's lips rose evenly at both corners when he grinned. "Precious is very good at her work. I've never met someone with as much patience as her. She mentioned wanting to start her own business."

Osei's back went rigid, and his ears prickled with interest. "Pardon me?"

His father picked up the squishy ball on the side table with his right hand and transferred it to his left. He squeezed and released it. "She felt guilty about missing the appointment with me and explained that she'd been upset after having been declined a loan."

Osei fought to hide his shock by nodding in understanding while keeping his face in a neutral expression.

"That's good. She seems like she enjoys her job," he said when he wanted to ask his father a million questions about what else Precious had told him. They communicated, but she hadn't shared anything personal about herself since they'd gotten together.

Have you poured out your hopes, dreams, and aspirations to her? Told her something about yourself she couldn't discover by asking a family member?

He slammed the thought down with a blink and focused on trying to influence his father into sharing more about Precious.

The older man flexed his left arm so his hand touched his shoulder and slowly lowered it to the chair. The strength was returning, and they had both Precious and his father's stubborn will to thank for that. "My walking is coming along well. I'm even able to take steps with the walker."

Osei let his heart speak. "I'm proud of you, Dada. You've always been my inspiration and role model, but now..." He cleared the emotion from his throat. "You've proven just how strong an Aboagye can be."

His father raised a flexed fist and held it out before lowering it.

"With determination. Yes, but I couldn't have done it without my family." He looked directly at Osei. "Thank you, son."

He sat with his father for a few minutes before getting to his feet. Hanging around long enough to meet up with Precious would be a horrible idea. He could barely contain himself when he merely thought about her. Being in the same room would pinpoint to anyone present that they were involved when he found it impossible to not touch or look at her.

"Whoever she is, Osei, treat her well. The Aboagye obstinance is not always an easy thing to handle. Never be too proud. And learn from this old man that when you remain faithful to a woman, the abundance of blessings she brings will be more than any skirt you can chase."

He hadn't been around during his father's wilder days when he'd initially gotten married to his mother. Not one to tolerate anyone's nonsense, with her family's support, she'd given his father a choice of having her or other women. Four college-educated children, a home in a great area, a successful business, a master's degree, and a retired headmaster position at a prestigious secondary school in Accra, her unyielding support and daily doses of happiness proved he'd made the right choice.

Their lives as husband and wife hadn't been perfect, but Osei knew he wanted a marriage like theirs when the time came. With open communication being the most important thing they shared.

"Thank you, Dada," he said without denying Precious one last time.

They weren't sneaking around, nor were they out in the open dating either. He couldn't introduce her to his parents without major ramifications. Yet, even having known her for all of six weeks, he could see things progressing between them past the casual status they were in now.

"Osei, one last thing."

"Yes, Dada."

"Be happy. Life is short, and you only get one so make the best out of it."

Would his father be singing the same song if he let him know Precious was the one making him grin as if he'd won the lottery every day? Doubtful. "Thank you. Have a good day, Dada."

How did he want to live his life? Working excessively until the stress of it hit him with an illness like it did his father? Or enjoying it by doing what he loved and being with a woman who made him feel special and wanted?

His heart thudded hard against his ribs as Precious' face miraged its way into his sight. She was everything he wanted in a woman and more. If only she weren't an Ewe.

Chapter Seventeen

Precious scooted the few inches it took to paste her back to her lover's chest after an enthusiastic session of sex where she'd taken control and ridden him. The room lay still as his even breathing and arm holding her close created a sense of security and rightness. Her raw need to be with a man had never been as strong as with Osei. Her core throbbed as she calculated how much time he'd need to recover before they did it again.

He'd surprised her with a visit on a Monday after he'd left her home the previous evening. Osei had yet to spend the night. It made her miserable to wave goodbye to him, but she understood. Their arrangement wasn't about cuddling and pillow talk. It definitely wasn't about him sleeping over. Not when he still lived at home and would have to justify where he'd been.

The acceptable reason for him leaving her bed didn't make her feel any better when in his arms was the only place she wanted to be these days. Her weekends belonged to him. Part of them, anyway. They both worked on Saturday mornings. From her assessment of Mr Aboagye's progression, she predicted she wouldn't need to work with him on such an intensive level for much longer. She'd miss him and the family when the time came to discharge him from her services.

Precious couldn't bring herself to contemplate what would happen between her and Osei. The thought of it created a hollowness which hadn't been there before he'd entered her life. They needed an end date so she could pick up the pieces when he was gone and move forward.

Osei's lips brushed against her bare shoulder. "Are you sleeping?"

"No. Doing a little thinking."

He stiffened behind her, but not in the way she enjoyed.

"What about?" His voice sounded tight.

She rolled until she faced him, adjusting the sheet to cover her breasts. "Are you okay?"

"Yes. Why?"

Realizing what was concerning him, she gathered her inner strength, prepared to keep things between them simple and not have their relationship implode before she was ready to let him go.

"Don't worry, what we have is still the same. Purely physical. What's in my brain doesn't concern you." She raised her foot and caressed it over his calf, the curly hair tickling as she pinned him with her gaze. "What's between my legs, on the other hand, is totally yours to focus on."

To emphasize her point, she pressed her mouth against his and teased until he took control. When he ended the kiss, they were both breathing hard, and she was on the cusp of admitting she'd grown some unexpected and unwarranted feelings for him.

Osei lay on his side, his head propped with one hand while the other caressed her arm. "I'd like to know more about you."

Her brows slammed together. "Where is this coming from, Osei?"

"My father mentioned this morning you wanted to start your own business, but you couldn't get the loan."

Her mouth dropped open. She hadn't bound Mr Aboagye to a confidentiality clause, but it stunned her those two had spoken about her. "How did that come up?"

"He was bragging about how good you are at your job and then told me why you had cancelled the only session you'd ever missed."

"I see." The conversation was becoming more intimate than the sex they'd been enjoying, and she couldn't allow it. Not if she wanted to survive intact when what they had ended. "I'm feeling sweaty so I'm going to bathe. When you're ready, you can see yourself out."

She went to swing her legs over the side of the bed, but he tugged at her arm.

"Can we talk?"

He sounded so serious, she wanted to say no. Her heart fluttered in fear. Was he going to break up with her right then? Whatever needed discussing, they'd do it dressed and in the hall.

"Sure. After I get washed." When he went to speak, she put up a finger. "Alone. You should put your clothes on."

His frown was replaced with a brisk nod. "Okay."

No longer shy when it came to being naked around Osei, she got out of bed and sauntered to the bathroom.

If he was going to end their arrangement, she'd give him something to regret leaving.

***

Osei sat in the hall brooding, a cup of tea on the coffee table as if he were in his own home. Being with Precious felt just as comfortable. Why did he have to ruin a fun evening by trying to become serious? What did it matter if she hadn't told him about her struggles? They were meant to appease each other sexually. Not to console.

But the way she'd jumped right in to remind him about the nature of their relationship had his stomach plummeting. Was he the only one catching feelings? He hadn't bargained for it, but something in him had known from their first conversation that she was special. His resistance had been destroyed with an invitation to lunch that he often smiled about, because it had transformed his life. Precious had changed him. He hadn't worked on a Sunday in the full month they'd been together, which made him more relaxed and happier in general.

She came out of her room wearing a pair of mid-thigh shorts and a T-shirt, and smelling of cocoa butter. She sat on the armchair adjacent to him.

"Can I make you a cup of tea?" he offered.

Her features softened from that of a stern teacher about to punish a misbehaving student into a smile. "No, thank you."

Raising his cup, he took a sip of his own without cringing at the unsweetened peppermint flavour. His stomach had been tied in knots ever since she'd basically kicked him out of her home earlier. Time to be open and honest. "I'm feeling lost right now."

Brows rose on a make-up free face. "How so?"

"Regardless of how much we talk and our sexual intimacy, I don't know a lot about you. Well, not the important things such as you wanting to open your own rehabilitation centre. It threw me to learn it from my father."

"That's the kind of situationship we have. Casual. Remember?"

It was as if she'd thrown the knife into his chest while taking a running start. He moved over to the end of the couch closest to her.

"I want to get to know you. All of you. To understand what you're going through and to share my experiences with you." Unnerved by her unreadable expression as she considered him, he continued. "I'd like for us to date and see where this thing between us will go."

She altered her position to lean forward with her elbows on her knees. What had he expected? For her to jump up and hug him in celebration? That wasn't the kind of person she was. Intentional. She did everything with consideration and purpose, which was why he feared her response.

If she had no feelings for him, then he would've complicated the relationship, and she'd boot him out with her next words. Even if her emotions had gotten as tangled as his, it didn't mean she wanted more from him.

"What would this mean?"

He released a breath realizing she hadn't declined his proposal outright. "That we be exclusive. Get to know each other with the purpose of seeing where it takes us."

"I'm going to be honest." She tucked her lips into her mouth, looked to the side, took a deep breath, and returned her gaze. "You're the first Akan man I have ever been involved with."

She was the first Ewe woman for him, but he'd keep it locked away. If she agreed, he'd have to find a way to ease her into his father's good graces. The man would have to be heartless to be tribalistic towards a woman he respected. Which he was far from.

"Why?" he asked, wanting to know if it had been deliberate. She'd gone to KNUST in the Ashanti Region which consisted of students from the broader Akan ethnic group, but the university drew in people from all over Ghana, even the world. Being an outgoing, beautiful woman, she'd probably had her pick of men.

"My father's name was Kwame Asante Agyekum Gyasi."

His body ceased to move as shock took over. And then the memory of her words hit. "Was it his side of the family you used to visit in Beposo when you were a child?"

She sat up straight as her eyes widened. "You remember?"

"Yes." If she knew how closely he paid attention to her words and mannerisms, she'd understand how much she'd bored into his heart already. He'd committed how she looked when she was in the throes of an orgasm to memory. He found everything she did to be worth remembering.

"My father was an Ashanti and my mother an Ewe who grew up in a village near Keta. They attended Secondary School in Koforidua and met at a church social gathering. They were inseparable ever since. At least, that's what they used to tell me." She grinned. "Selorm said they had a few breakups along the way, but ended up together despite the challenges. One of those issues was that neither of their families accepted the other."

She let the words permeate. "My mother supported my father when he decided to attend vocational school to become a mechanic. He reciprocated when she went to learn how to be a hair dresser. I was born sometime in between those years, but before then, they'd accepted that they would never have their family's support and married in the courts with distant cousins as witnesses. Their families eventually allowed them back into the fold, but when my parents died, neither side claimed me."

"Lineage," Osei said in horrified understanding.

"Lineage," she repeated. "If it hadn't been for the woman I now call my mother, I would've been on my own despite having two families, whose blood runs through me."

He couldn't imagine what that must've felt like. To be dismissed as not belonging. The comment she'd started out with made complete sense as full comprehension dawned. "You relate to your Ewe side because of Aunty Selorm. You've shunned the Ashanti side of you because you never want your children to experience what you did."

The tear slipped down her cheek before she could get up and walk to the kitchen.

His heart broke for the girl she'd been and the woman she'd become. How could she ever trust that his family, although matrilineal by culture, would never deny a child they would produce? The little remarks his father had made about the Ewe people over the years pinged in his head, and he was no longer sure they wouldn't.

Chapter Eighteen

Why hadn't she just let her instincts rule her response and told him she also wanted more? Because life was one big ball of pain sometimes, and she couldn't let her moments of happiness obliterate the potential for misery if something were to go wrong.

But what about his father?

After the comment she'd overheard Mr Aboagye make on the phone when she'd walked into the house the week she'd first started, about Ewe students overrunning the universities of Ghana, she'd understood his stance on her people. Although he'd been friendly, cooperative, and not in the least bit antagonist towards her, she sensed it came because they shared a professional relationship. He needed her as a therapist and respected her as one.

If she and Osei became exclusive, it would become personal. For all of them. What would that mean for Osei? Or had she misinterpreted his father's words?

She'd just spilled her heart out to him about the greatest loss she'd ever faced. Her life had been heavily influenced by her parents, both their lives and deaths.

He had a right to know. The lie didn't sit well with her conscience. She desperately wanted to be with him, but the threat of inevitable agony and rejection perpetually hung over her like a storm cloud. Her admission had been meant to remind her of why they shouldn't be together, but it hadn't worked.

Grabbing a sachet of water from the refrigerator, she took a careful sip to clear the lump from her throat as she wiped the tears away with the back of her hand. She had no idea why she was crying. She'd gotten over her loss years ago and thought of her parents and childhood with fondness.

Having the reason why she'd stayed away from Ashanti men flung at her with brutal honesty by a man from that tribe had been hard. Not at all the same as when Lamisi, Toyin, or even her mother did it.

Here was a man asking to be with her. Someone she got along with and longed to be around, but the stumbling blocks were massive. She doubted her strength to handle them.

"Precious?"

She looked up to find Osei a few feet away with his arms outstretched. Accepting the invitation, she stepped into his embrace and clung.

Large hands rubbing her back comforted. She sank deeper into him as she inhaled his scent. Not just his cologne, but the light musk of his skin after making love proved an aphrodisiac she craved to bottle and keep for those times he wasn't around.

"I understand why you might be afraid to get involved with me." His voice rumbled into her. "I've heard some horrid stories where intertribal relationships didn't survive." He squeezed her a little tighter. "I've heard even more successful ones. It depends on the individuals and how hard they're willing to fight for what they want."

She leaned back against his arms to look into his eyes. "My story is different. It wasn't about my parents' relationship not working out. It was because it did, and then they died and left me." Alone.

His eyes held an earnest sorrow. "You have my condolences on the loss of your parents. It must've been difficult to lose them at such a young age."

"It was. They were so full of life. All I remember is how much they loved each other. And me." Her voice trembled. "They loved me so much."

"I'm sure they did. Even though you were most likely a troublemaker."

She snorted. "No, sir. By your admission, that was you. I was an angel, wings and all."

"Ha," he teased. "Now I know you're lying."

She giggled. "I was a handful. My mother gave up on calling me Precious and made my full name her go-to. That's when I could no longer differentiate if they'd discovered what I'd gotten into."

"What is your full name?"

"Precious Asantewaa. My last name used to be Gyasi until I changed it to Kpodo to match the woman who adopted me. It made life a lot easier to have people think she was my biological mother. And with the wonderful way she raised me, no one questioned it."

"Aunty Selorm took care of me before she did you."

If she hadn't been looking into his face, she'd have sworn he'd stuck out his tongue. "She took pity on a mischievous rat. That's the kind of big-hearted woman she is."

"Do you think we would've gotten along if we'd met back then?"

"No." She didn't hesitate to answer. "I would've been jealous of you and the attention my mother threw your way even though you had parents at home. I was a spoiled princess. I still am." She tapped her chin, holding back a grin. "I'm astonished we get along now."

He bent and skimmed his lips against a spot just behind her ear. "Are you really?"

Tilting her head to the side, she moaned as he nipped the sensitive skin. He knew just where to touch to give maximum pleasure. Pushing against his shoulders, she put space between them. "We were having a serious conversation."

His gaze focused on her lips. "We were?"

Taking a few steps back so they were no longer touching, she leaned against the counter. "I recall you asking to date me. Exclusively."

"I like that you have a good memory."

If she was going to do this, she'd have to put aside her old trauma and trust that everything would work out. That he'd be worth it. Was this how her mother had felt when she'd met her father? As if nothing else in the world mattered except being with him? Precious would never get the chance to ask her, but she had the opportunity to see where her relationship with Osei would lead. Even if it hit a brick wall and shattered her, she'd appreciate the time she'd spend with him because he was becoming important to her.

She took in a deep breath of certainty and exhaled any lingering doubts. If only life were that easy to control. Ready to take a leap of faith, she nodded. "Yes."

In a flash, she was lifted onto the counter, her legs wrapped around his waist. Peppermint infused her taste buds as his tongue did magnificent things to her mouth.

Panting, Osei pulled back. "If I had a condom, I'd take you right here."

She tugged at the hem of the work shirt she'd almost torn off of him when he'd walked into her home a few hours ago.

"Lucky us, then." She tipped to the side and opened an overhead cabinet. "Look in the corner behind the coffee on the right, there's a small bag."

"You don't drink coffee," he said as he hunted for their treasure.

The button of his trousers released easily enough. From experience, she knew the zipper would be the tricky part. "Neither do the people who regularly visit me. It's exactly why I keep a secret stash of protection behind the cannister."

She divested him of his pants, gliding her fingers along his length. If he didn't hurry, she'd jump down and cover him with her mouth. She knew just how he liked to be sucked and licked. How deep she could take him as he grabbed the back of her head. How he tasted as he came in her mouth.

He groaned as she rimmed the bulbous dark tip.

The ripping of a packet grabbed her attention, and she released him. Maintaining her position, she shimmied out of her shorts and panties until they hit the floor. Heads bent, she watched as he scooted her to the edge of the counter and then entered her.

The moans came simultaneously as he pushed in. Their eyes caught and held as he stayed still, their bodies joined in a manner familiar, exciting, and yet different.

"Precious." He ground his hips against her, hitting her in the perfect spot to make her hiss. "My woman."

"Yes. Now give me what I need."

"Say it first."

If she wasn't desperate, she'd hold out. Tell a few jokes even, but she was wet, throbbing, and ready for him to set the rhythm that would send them both spiralling into bliss. "My man. My exceptional lover. My—"

His lips crashed onto hers as his hips gave her just what she needed. Nothing felt as good as Osei filling her. Her whimper got lost in his mouth as she took him in over and over again. Knowing this was the first time they made love as a committed couple heightened the sensations of their joining with more intensity than ever before.

"Osei. Baby." She'd held back so many times from calling him anything other than his name. Now that he was hers, she was free. "Faster. Yes. Right there."

It wasn't long before she tasted the saltiness at the crook of his neck where she muffled her cry of release. She held tight as his powerful thrusts brought on his climax, seeming to fill her even further.

Time stopped as they held each other. He slid out, but kept his arms around her. The hardness of the countertop came into her awareness. She wasn't sure she'd be able to walk, but was ready to try.

"Sweetheart, wrap your legs around me and hold on."

Trusting his strength, she did what he requested. Her man carrying her after making love to her in a way that had left her wondering if gravity still existed had to be the most spectacular thing she'd ever experienced.

He laid her on her bed and kissed her lightly on the forehead. "I'll be right back to clean you."

She grew so overwhelmed, she couldn't breathe. This wasn't the first time he'd shown how sweet he could be, but it impressed none-the-less.

When he returned, he held their discarded clothes in one hand and a washcloth and towel in the other. He took his time wiping her down and drying her. When he looked at her panties, he thought better of putting them on her as he saw how wet they were. He went to her lingerie drawer to pull out another pair.

To her surprise, he chose a pair of cotton briefs. "No thong?"

"I like to peel those off of you." He waved the item in the air. "I wouldn't know first-hand, but I'd think these are more comfortable."

"You're definitely not wrong." She lifted her hips as he finished dressing her.

They lay facing each other, their fingers entwined. He'd have to leave soon no matter how much she wanted him to stay.

"Why do you still live with your parents?" she asked, successful at keeping the whine out of her voice.

Laughing, he raised her hand to his mouth and kissed her knuckles. "How long have you been holding that in?"

"Since I learned you still live with them."

"As you very well know, culturally, we reside with our parents until we're married."

"Not all of us. I love my mother, but freedom and ruling my own home is good. I couldn't shake the taste of independence I got when at university."

He nodded. "Me, too. But there are too many benefits to staying at home for me to ignore. The main ones being that I save money, and they let me use their garage as my workshop." He held up a finger. "But number one is my mother's cooking."

"Do you cook?"

"The question is, did my mother make sure none of her children would be reliant on anyone else for their sustenance?"

Her shoulders shook with silent laughter. "Is that a yes or no?"

"I cook. Clean. Wash. Pound and turn fufu, but not at the same time."

"You're making yourself sound like the perfect man."

Osei stroked a finger along her cheek. "Hopefully, for you, I am."

Her smile broadened. So far, he seemed to be, but only time would tell. If they were to proceed as a couple, she needed to share the most important goal she'd ever undertaken. She was ready to let him in.

So she told him about her passion project of opening a rehabilitation centre. The most difficult part was sharing about being rejected by every bank she'd applied to. All in, she trusted him not to judge her as a complete failure, so she did it.

"Have you applied for a loan from Allegiant Bank? I could put in a good word for you."

The nature of his work was to be a fixer, but that wasn't what she required from him. His support would be enough.

"It was the first bank I applied to. I'm going to postpone starting my business for now." She placed a finger over his lips when he started to speak. "I've thought a lot about it, and I've decided it's the best option for me right now. I'm not letting go of my dream, just delaying it for a little while. Maybe I'll find a partner or investors one day."

"It's a wise decision. Especially in this economy."

She assessed him through squinted eyes. "No further advice or contributions?"

"Would you listen or get angry?"

He really knew her, it seemed. "Not get angry, but annoyance would hit."

"Then no. I learn lessons very quickly. I figure you'll ask if you want my opinion."

That's the moment she fell in love with him. A hard drop that left her breathless, disbelieving, and yet sure at the same time. She cleared her throat once she'd been able to suck in oxygen. "Smart man."

She desperately hoped she could say the same about herself. Osei was a great man who came from a good family, but in the back of her mind was the question of them accepting her, an Ewe, half anyway, with their oldest son. An even stronger fear hit when she thought about what would happen if they had children and both of them ended up dying.

No.

She wouldn't allow such negativity to invade. Her parents' past was not her future. She had her own life to live, and being with Osei made her happy. It was only a matter of seeing where the relationship would take them.

Chapter Nineteen

"Thanks for inviting us to the party. Toyin became incredibly jealous when I told him where I was going tonight. If he hadn't travelled for work, he'd probably have sewn himself to my dress. I can't wait to boast about everyone I saw here. He might never speak to me again," Precious gushed to Lamisi as they sipped drinks in the lavish five-star hotel ballroom.

The guests, dressed in their glamourous finest, dazzled. Some women wore prints in styles that were the least traditional she'd ever seen, with the backs of the dresses missing and deep, plunging necklines. Others went the fashion route of the West with sparkling sheath dresses or ball gowns she could recall seeing on television during the American high school season of proms.

Precious had opted for the maroon and silver kaba and slit combination she'd worn as a maid-of-honour to Lamisi's wedding. No one would ever recall it because her friend had outshone everyone on that day.

Lamisi took a sip of her drink. "I don't think I'll ever get used to being around so many people. Blaise is even worse than me, so he's no help. I had to encourage him to attend. Exposure and all that."

Precious sighed. "I still get star-struck whenever I'm with Blaise and his cohort. In one room, we have hiplife and highlife artists intermingling as if they're regular people. And don't get me started on these huge actors and comedians. My neck hurts from every time I snap my head around to gawk."

Lamisi giggled. "They have neck braces in the first-aid area just in case of whiplash."

"Smart move." Precious got distracted as a voluptuous woman in a stunning navy blue dress floated past her. "Is that Phyllis Quarshie?"

If she had the courage, she'd walk over to her favourite actress and, well, probably squeal like she was on the verge of doing now.

Lamisi grabbed Precious' hand. "Yes. And you need to calm down before you embarrass us both. There won't be a repeat of the time you met Majestic."

Taking a gulp of her drink, she controlled her excitement. "I blame you for not letting me tag along with you and Blaise for these special events more often. This is amazing. All for a great cause. Artists for Orphans will help so many children."

"Indeed. Omar Fosu is an incredibly generous man. Blaise was the one who went ballistic when Omar asked him to sit on the foundation's board."

The highlife artist had grown up as an orphan and bypassed the poverty he might have been destined for if he hadn't fought so hard to get out. Now, he helped others. Thinking of how close she'd come to being an orphan, she'd be sure to donate to the worthy cause.

Precious scanned the crowd, looking for the man she'd arrived with. They'd been late because as soon as he'd shown up at her door, clothes had come off and been carefully placed before they'd had sex that still caused her face to become flushed. In the three weeks of being labelled as exclusive, she couldn't get over how fantastic it felt to claim him as her man.

When Osei looked up from the conversation he held with Blaise, piercing eyes landed on her as if he'd known where she was the whole time. His smile set off a flutter in her belly, and she sighed.

"Things look like they're going well between you two." Lamisi had given her approval when the four of them had gone to lunch last Sunday.

"I can't believe that I'm with him. He's so good to me."

Lamisi grunted. "He'd better be."

"He hasn't told his family about us." Because he respected his parents' opinions so much, she got the sense it was the one thing that could tear them apart and she was scared.

"Have you told Aunty Selorm?"

"No. She'd start planning a wedding right away. And begin demanding grandchildren. I want to be sure it's heading in that direction with Osei."

"And him introducing you to his family as his partner would cement it."

She raised a finger towards the glistening chandelier. "Exactly."

"Be patient," Lamisi said in a calm, reassuring voice. "He'll introduce you when the time is right."

"What if they don't accept me?"

Lamisi frowned. "But you said they love working with you."

"There's a big difference with me getting their father to be mobile and independent, and me dating their first born. Me, an Ewe—"

"Half Ashanti, half Ewe."

Precious lifted an exposed shoulder and let it drop. "Same difference. Since I was raised by an Ewe woman, they'll see me as one."

"What would you tell me if I were in your situation?"

She didn't even have to think about it. "To enjoy the present and not worry about the future because everything will work out fine." She monotoned the words she'd have put more emphasis into if she were advising her friend.

Lamisi clinked their glasses. "I remember hearing something similar when I was worried about Blaise, and look how well it turned out."

Precious raised a brow, reminding Lamisi she'd been there for the whole adventure of that unexpected romance.

"Okay," Lamisi added. "It wasn't smooth sailing, but here we are happy and together. You just have to be patient. Don't try to force it."

"Fine."

"Good." Lamisi looped their arms. "Let's join our men. The hiplife and highlife grooves the DJ is playing are making me want to dance."

"Me, too. Look who just walked in," she screeched while staring at the door. "If I wasn't with Osei, I'd shoot my shot with—"

"Majestic." Lamisi completed.

The friends giggled and headed to the men they'd be going home with.

***

The tightness of his lower back muscles reminded Osei that he'd been stooped over for much too long. He examined the piece of reclaimed wood he was working with. It had insisted on becoming a small centre table when he'd planned for it to be a double-tiered stand.

He'd missed creating, using the salvaged wood of felled trees and cast-off timber to make items for people to appreciate in their homes. Merging the wood with metal, glass, and whatever he could add to enhance the product's design brought a sense of satisfaction.

The low inventory he had in stock had reminded him that he needed to get some work done if he was to have anything to sell at the next market day in two weeks.

He turned when he sensed a presence at the door of the garage. Precious stood staring at him, and his heart banged in his chest as if trying to reach her. "Hi."

"Hi."

Her smile alone could heal—no wonder his father was getting more mobile so easily. "You've finished with my father?"

"Yes. Our last Saturday session. We'll only meet in the mornings now, which I've reduced to three times a week, for fine-tuning and strength-building."

"It amazes me to see him walking around the house with a cane." His movements were slow and careful, but he'd reached his goal of being more independent.

She looked around his workspace. "So, this is where all the woodworking magic happens."

"I wouldn't call it magic, but yes."

Stepping into the space, she touched the piece he'd been working on.

His skin tingled, longing to experience her caress. "It still needs to be stained."

She went to a pile of wood he kept in the corner. "One day, I'd like to see you make something from the very beginning."

"It would be boring to just observe."

Her gaze roamed from his eyes, over his tank top-covered chest, lingering at his exposed arms before grazing down his legs and then back up again. "I doubt it."

At the huskiness in her voice, he rushed over and backed her into the wall before lowering his head to capture her lips.

Her arms wrapped around his shoulders as she opened her mouth to allow him entry. The sweetness of having her so close in a place where he did what he loved made him lightheaded, and he lost all track of time and space. He belonged with Precious and would do anything to keep her with him.

A clearing of someone's throat registered, and reality hit. He pulled away and turned to face the intruder while hiding his woman behind his back. He might look to be protecting her dignity, but he still hadn't told his family about their relationship, and he didn't need them to find out this way.

Not only one, but both of his sisters stood grinning at the doorway.

"Hi, Precious," Serwaa and Dorcas said at the same time.

Precious stepped out from behind him. "Hello. I've bought a few things from Osei at the Blue Leaf Market and since he was at home for once while I was here, I wanted to see his work station." She turned her attention to him. "Thank you."

Her rambled explanation wasn't fooling anyone, especially not his sisters.

"Yes, he's very talented. We all think he should do it as a full-time business," Dorcas said.

"Not Dada, though," Serwaa added. "And his approval is most important to Osei despite having everyone else's support. Which he has."

"Because he deserves to be happy," Dorcas concluded with the same goofy smile that appeared when she watched videos of puppies and kittens.

As if intuiting that his siblings were referring to more than his furniture-making, Precious pointed to the open space where she'd obtain freedom. "I need to go. Have a good day."

Osei took a step forward. "I'll see you out."

"No. I will," Serwaa said with a warning look thrown in his direction. "I'll be right back."

Her code for not starting the conversation about what they'd witnessed before she returned rang loud and clear.

Why had he been so stupid? The garage was in full view of the kitchen window. Now that his father was up and about, if he'd decided to go in there for whatever reason, they'd have been caught.

Maybe it's what he'd subconsciously wanted. He was tired of hiding the most special person he'd ever met. Having his sisters find him with Precious could only mean one thing. Time to expose their relationship to his parents.

Chapter Twenty

The most vociferous member of the family stormed into the shed and closed the door, trapping the three of them in. Everyone thought Serwaa was the oldest until otherwise informed of Osei's status as the first born.

She placed her hands on her hips. "How could you? Right in the open like that for anyone to see," she said in Twi.

Dorcas joined ranks with her older sister. "As if Precious is one of your last-for-a-week women for you to treat anyhow."

Not understanding what was going on, his gaze swung between the women.

"She's friendly, intelligent, and funny. That's a perfect combination," Serwaa said with a nod.

"And she doesn't take nonsense," Dorcas added. "You should've heard the way she dealt with a nurse who was being rude to Dada when he was in the hospital. Tactful, yet direct. I almost applauded."

Serwaa turned to Dorcas. "The nurse's mumbled apology did it for me. She'll make a wonderful sister. She'll have our backs. Plus her style is amazing. You should've seen what she was wearing at the Achimota

Mall when I ran into her last month. I need to borrow that dark green wraparound skirt. And she was so easy to talk to during our impromptu lunch."

The conversation had swept him away to a place where confusion and ignorance led the pack.

"It's her confidence I appreciate most," Serwaa continued. "I haven't tried to analyse her, but so far, there are no psychological issues I've detected." The mental health nurse turned therapist never shut off, so she'd probably assessed Precious during every encounter. His sister shook her head. "I'll never understand how Osei impressed her enough to give him a chance."

They swivelled to him, the intensity in their identical eyes disconcerting.

Serwaa crossed her arms over her chest. "I don't think you deserve her. Not with how much you work. When will you make time to treat her the way she deserves to be pampered?"

Dorcas flung her waist-length cornrow extensions over her shoulder. "I was thinking of introducing her to Isaac if things don't work out between her and Osei. She'd still be part of the family. A cousin-in-law isn't as tight as a sister, but at least, we wouldn't lose her."

"It's a good idea," Serwaa agreed. "Isaac is a good choice personality-wise, and he has enough money to lavish her while being able to spend time with her. But she'd probably move to Kumasi if they got married. That would defeat the purpose."

"Maybe we could convince—"

Osei held up both hands.

"Enough." He had to gain control of the situation before it spiralled further out of hand. "I'm your brother. Aren't you supposed to be on my side?"

"We are," Dorcas said. "That's why we're ecstatic you and Precious are together."

"We don't want you to mess it up and drive her away."

Confusion lingered. "How did you know we're dating? Did Precious tell you?"

"No." Dorcas waved a hand. "We like her, but we aren't close like that."

"Yet," Serwaa tagged on.

The sisters shared a high five followed by a hip bump.

They were giving him an ulcer. "How did you know?"

"We saw you sitting at the Kotanga Hotel's pool area a few weeks ago," Serwaa answered. "As soon as we recognized you two dancing to the live band, looking more into each other than friends would be, we left."

Dorcas tapped her chest. "I wanted to say hello and stay. The band was on fire. Serwaa dragged me out. The next place we went wasn't anywhere as good, but we managed to make the best of it."

"Don't worry. We haven't told anyone. Except for Bismark. Baby bro likes that you're no longer on his neck about his own choices now that you're occupied with…" Serwaa cleared her throat. "Other things."

Ready to leave the conversation about him and Precious, he took the opportunity to change the subject. "He needs to do something with his degree. He can't work at Mama's shop all his life."

"Let him do what he wants. If it's good enough for Mama, then it's good enough for your brother. He's even expanded the shop." Serwaa waved her hand as if flicking something away. "You can't distract us from the real issue, Osei. Things could've gone badly if it had been Mama coming out to find you. We stopped her just in time when we noticed the direction Precious had headed."

Dorcas tilted her head. "What are you going to do about Dada?"

The question hit him square in the gut, and suddenly, the open window wasn't letting in enough air. The heat of the enclosed space started to suffocate him. He pushed the door open and walked onto the compound, the dry air grating his throat with each gulped inhale.

His sisters had followed him out.

Telling his father about Precious was his worst nightmare. He'd avoided thinking about it, hoping a miracle would make things work out without any intervention from him. He'd been a fool.

"I don't know," he answered once he'd calmed down.

Dorcas stood to his right in the small triangle they'd made. "I think because Dada likes and respects Precious, he'll accept her."

He turned away from the piteous understanding in Serwaa's eyes.

"Our father is a restrictive man when it comes to us dating Ewes," Serwaa reminded their younger sister.

Dorcas paced the small space they took up. "It doesn't make sense in this day and age to exclude anyone where love is concerned. Why is Dada like that?"

"He's never told us the full story, but he has mentioned that his life had once been at risk because of them when he was younger," Serwaa answered. "He got angry when he mentioned it, so I've never gotten up the courage to ask him. Not even when he told Bismark off once he'd discovered he'd been dating an Ewe."

Their brother hadn't been serious about the young woman from the Volta Region, so he hadn't had a problem ending the relationship. Osei wouldn't do it. Not with his heart now invested in Precious. He loved her. It had snuck up on him, but recognizing and accepting it made him happy. Whole.

He decided right then to invite Precious to a family dinner and inform his parents they were together. His father would be forced to accept her if everyone else did. His mother had no problems with who they dated as long as they were good people. His father was the only hurdle.

Osei would fight for Precious and make his father accept what they shared.

***

"I'd like to introduce you to my family. As my girlfriend."

Precious lowered the beef shawarma wrap midway to her mouth. This was the moment she'd been waiting for. Yesterday when Osei's sisters had caught them kissing, she'd freaked out. It had been a pivotal moment. One of revelation, and she'd been waiting for either this shoe to drop or the one where he broke up with her.

"Did Dorcas and Serwaa threaten to tell?" she inquired, forcing herself to stay calm. Running around the small restaurant shouting yes to meeting his family as his woman wouldn't be dignified.

"No. They'd already figured it out when they saw us at the Kotanga Hotel."

Her mind went to what a great time she'd had that night, both on and off the dance floor. "And they were okay about it?" She got along with his sisters as if they'd always been friends, but things could change once they discovered she was involved with their brother.

Osei's eyes sparkled. "They told me not to mess it up with you."

"They're the best. Your brother was cool the few times I met him, too. In fact, I like your whole family, but why introduce me now?"

"It's time they learned how serious I am about you. I'd like for them to get to know you as more than my father's physiotherapist."

She took a gulp of her Fanta to prevent proclaiming her love out loud. Yes, he cared about her, wanted to be with her, but did he love her? He hadn't said it, and she'd be darned if she'd be the one to let the words enter the atmosphere between them first. "I'd like to have dinner with your family. When?"

"My father mentioned you'd be finished with his physio in a couple of weeks."

"It's true. We've already reduced to three times a week only once a day. He's done so well. Today, we walked to the front of the compound with just the cane. Unless I want him carrying me around the house, there's not much more I can do for him. We're going to spend some time on the fine movements of his hand. He's right-handed, so he doesn't have to concern himself with learning how to write again, but it would be good to have a stronger grasp in the left."

He liked how animated and passionate she became while talking about her work. "A family celebration of his accomplishments would be a great reason for us all to come together."

"Sounds good. Let me know when it's coming on, and I'll be there." She went back to eating the spicy meal.

Osei looked beyond her with his brows furrowed. His pensive expression made the food sink like a boulder in her stomach. She tried to give him time to process whatever he was going through, but she couldn't take it anymore. "What's wrong?"

His sigh disturbed her more than the contemplative silence.

"My father," he paused and rubbed a hand over his head. "I don't know how to say this."

With the remainder of her meal now forgotten, Precious waited for him to find the words to let her know what she'd already suspected about his father's prejudice against Ewes. She'd never gotten the sense Osei believed any such nonsense his father probably did, but his family was close, and doing anything against his father's wishes could be detrimental to that relationship.

"My father can be..." he grunted. "Hell, he's bigoted against Ewes. Not in action, but in speech."

Which was just as bad. "What do you mean?"

"He'll treat everyone equally, but sometimes, he'll say unflattering things about them."

Mr Aboagye wasn't the first person she'd encountered with such an attitude, and if she hadn't already guessed it before, she'd be shocked. "But he's educated to the Master's level. And he's an educationist. Why?"

Osei shrugged. "We don't know. Not even my mother. He gets upset when anyone asks him, so we leave it alone."

"When he's being degrading, do you tell him it's wrong?"

The silence as he turned away from her probing gaze revealed the answer.

"We try. We'll say something discouraging, like 'Oh, Dada, that's not right to say.' No one chastises him like we should, but we don't encourage it either."

What could she say? At least, he'd been honest. Fear of losing Osei claimed the space optimism had a few moments ago. "Your father has treated me with nothing but deference, but how will he take it when you tell him we're together?"

His cheeks puffed out with a harsh exhale. "I don't know."

They sat in a tense bubble of silence the rest of the patrons in the restaurant weren't affected by.

"I'm hoping since he likes you, he'll be accepting."

She had no idea what he'd say, but knew the answer she wanted to hear, so the devil's advocate in her made her ask. "What would you do if he didn't?"

His eyes locked with hers.

"You're important to me, Precious." He paused. "And I'm a grown man. My father's opinion and support means a lot, but I won't allow anyone to tell me what I should do with my life. For the first time since university, I'd pack up and leave my father's house."

Her fingers flew to her lips as she gasped at his statement. "You don't mean that."

"I do."

"But what about your family?"

He shook his head. "I'd have to move out at some point. If my father can't accept my choices, then that's on him."

"But—"

"It is what it is. Are you ready to go? The movie starts in a few minutes."

She doubted she'd be able to focus on it. "Um, yes."

Heart heavy, she got to her feet. There was no more discussion to be had. She'd learned that once Osei was through talking about something, the topic was done. For the meantime. She'd also discovered that when she brought it up while he was relaxed, the discussion went smoother.

Creating a chasm between a man and his family wouldn't settle well within her. She had to decide if she was willing to be the cause of such a rift if his father didn't accept her. She had three weeks to make a decision.

Back out of the relationship and have her heart broken. Or hang in there with Osei knowing their involvement may ruin his family.

Chapter Twenty-One

"What do you think, Toyin?"

The decision about being introduced to Osei's family as his girlfriend loomed. The thought of it excited her, but the consequences of being denied brought on a panic that made her break out into a cold sweat. How long could they remain as they were, attempting to hide their relationship? His sisters had already seen them together and made a very correct assumption. Accra wasn't as big as people thought, especially when they all generally moved in the same areas.

And then the fact she loved Osei and wanted the ultimate commitment of marriage one day. She hadn't taken any of her former short-term relationships seriously enough to ever think about getting married. She'd given up on it, deciding to commit her attention and life to her career. She'd never guessed a day would come where she'd feel as if she were leaking light from the overabundance of joy at possibly sharing her life with the man she loved.

"You've decided to ask my opinion now?" Toyin asked, his tone dripping with attitude. "It's been over a week since he asked you, and now you come to me? Huh."

Precious took no offence to her friend's mild scolding. "I'm sure you would've answered my multiple calls if you hadn't decided to visit London with your new man."

"I've responded with texts. And he's not new. I feel as if our souls have known each other since the dawn of time," Toyin gushed. "I'd never believed in soul mates until him."

She grinned as he basked in the ecstasy of being in love. No denying the feeling of rightness when it came. "I'm happy for you. I've been keeping up with you on Insta. Hashtag London Baby has become your go-to."

"Gideon has been the perfect tour guide, showing me all the sights of his city. Gurrlll, why didn't you tell me London was the land of sexual freedom?"

She laughed. "Because I went to the UK for education."

It had surprised her at the time to see many people being so open about their sexuality and public displays of affection. Once the shock had worn off, it all became natural. "It's easier in the UK for people to be themselves, so I didn't pay any mind other than during LGBTQ+ Pride Month."

She'd become more aware of the struggle ever since becoming friends with Toyin and hearing about the things he'd gone through. She'd often wondered if they'd have become friends if she hadn't engaged with people in the LGBTQ+ community when she'd been in the UK.

"Pride Month! Yes, please."

Precious pulled the phone away as Toyin nearly blew her eardrum out.

"I'm returning just to celebrate it live and in person. I've never been able to show affection to my man in public without the threat of being beaten or killed, but here, even if we get looks, we're still safe. Mostly."

"Please be careful, Toyin. And don't get arrested for indecent exposure. It would take me too long to get a visa to get you out of jail."

His chuckle boomed. "Gideon's family would take care of us if that happened. They're so supportive. It's the most amazing feeling to be out and free. Granted, there are ignorant people here, too, but compared to Nigeria and Ghana…they don't even measure to a drop in the ocean."

"Do you think you'll move there?" She hoped the answer would be no because she'd miss him too much.

"Gideon's contract in Ghana is for another three years. He hasn't decided if he'll renew or not, but he's leaning towards it. Gold Meadows pays him big time as an expat mining engineer. He's thinking of making *all* that bank before leaving. He didn't grow up in Ghana, but he loves it now that he's there."

"Why wouldn't he?" she bragged. "Ghana is the best country in all of Africa."

"Don't start, Precious. Otherwise, I'll bring up how your jollof rice needs vast improvements to measure up to what we make in Nigeria. And you all move so slowly, you'd think the air is made of molasses rather than oxygen. No hustle or bustle."

"Hey, we're a relaxed and friendly people. It's what we're known for. What you love about living in *my* country."

"Touché. Anyway, back to you and Osei. What did Lamisi say?" Toyin asked. "By the way, you looked amazing in that one-piece purple bathing suit you wore at Blaise's pool party last week."

"Thanks. I wasn't sure about it because the thigh is cut so high and showed some of the flesh of my stomach."

"Don't be crazy. You have a fabulous body. Healthy."

Heat rose to her face as she remembered all the times Osei had kissed and gripped the fleshy parts of her as they'd made love. He'd adored her body, making her feel special and wanted.

"Hey, Precious, are you still there?"

"Yes." She snapped out of her thoughts. "Did you say something?"

"I asked what Lamisi said about the situation."

"You know her. Follow your heart and blah blah blah." She stood and walked to the kitchen. "I need some definitive advice. What would you do if you were in my position?"

"You already know. That's why you're asking me."

Pouring guava juice into a glass, she nodded. "You'd say screw it and go for love. It wouldn't be your fault if a family was torn apart. The father shouldn't be tribalistic in the first place. This is the twenty-first century, after all."

"Damn straight. Despite what happens in movies, love doesn't come around easily. Compatibility is important, and once you find someone you match with, hold onto them and develop the relationship. Things won't be perfect, but they sure as hell will be good. His father made his bed, and if he wants his son in his life, then he needs to change the sheets. Your compassion for people is a lot more than mine. So how do you feel about the situation?"

She returned to the hall and placed the glass on one of Osei's coasters. The memories they'd made together shone throughout her home. "I love him, but at the same time, I know how important family is, and I don't want him to miss out on having a relationship with his father."

"But that's his choice to make, not yours."

If only it were that simple. "My head understands, but it doesn't stop me from feeling bad about the stress it's causing Osei. How can we be happy if he loses a huge part of him?"

"What about you, Precious? You've finally opened your heart to love, and here it is clear as day that it's entered your life. You deserve to be happy."

She sat up straight. "Do you think he's in love with me?"

"Precious! I know for a fact you aren't stupid. The man offered to leave his home if his father didn't accept you. If that isn't love, I don't know what is."

"But—"

"Just because he hasn't said it doesn't mean he doesn't feel it. Look at you. Have you told him yet?"

"No, but—"

"Precious, you're one of the boldest people I know. If you haven't said it to him, then there's an element of fear. Trust me, he feels the same about you. Be free. Be courageous and let him know."

"But—"

"Nope," Toyin interfered yet again. "You asked for my advice, and I gave it. What you do with it is up to you. You'd better be smart and take it. Now tell me what you want me to bring you home as a souvenir."

Where had the men in her life learned how to end a conversation so effectively? She needed to take notes and apply it to the rambling doubts in her head.

Toyin was right. She didn't even need to ask her mother where she stood on the subject. One of her many proverbs came to mind. *When one is in love, a mountain top becomes a flat field.*

She finally understood the meaning. The love she shared with Osei would help them get through anything that tried to get in their way. There was nothing to do but what Lamisi suggested and follow her heart.

Chapter Twenty-Two

Osei had insisted on picking Precious up from her apartment. They'd make a united front when walking into his family's home. His mother had asked fifty questions when he'd told her he'd be bringing a guest for dinner, but he'd sidestepped them all with vague answers.

His father had smirked and said, "It's about time we get to meet her."

The courage he thought he'd gathered to ask his father about his bias against Ewes had failed every time he'd gone to enquire. As effective as he was with making things happen and problem-solving at work, his father had a hold on him he found difficult to release.

Being with Precious made him feel like he could do anything. That's how he knew she was the one for him. How he understood holding on to their relationship, no matter how his father reacted, would be the best decision of his life.

Parking the car outside of the gate, he turned to Precious. "Are you ready?"

She grabbed his hand and squeezed. "Everything will be okay."

It had to be. He leaned over and kissed her on the cheek. They got out of the vehicle and went to the house. He opened the door and swept out his arm to let her in.

Seated in the hall, his father was the first to see Precious, and a broad grin revealed his pleasure.

She went to him. "Good evening, Mr Aboagye."

"Good evening, Precious. What are you doing here?"

Then with the speed of a flash flood, the corners of his mouth turned downward, and his eyes hardened. The room turned frigid with his sudden animosity as he picked up his cane, stood, and limped away without a word.

Precious turned to Osei, and his heart broke at the misery in her eyes compounded with his own disappointment.

Alone in the room, he went to her and caressed her bare arm.

"My father doesn't do well with surprises. That's all. After working with teenagers for years and raising four children, he really should be more accustomed to them. He'll come to accept us," he said as much for his benefit as hers.

She touched a hand to his chest, over his heart. Could she feel how fast it was beating with the combination of nerves and being close to her? She affected him with a force he'd never experienced before.

"I hope so," she said in a near whisper.

They seemed to be living in a perpetual state of hope where his father was concerned. Certainty was where he preferred to reside.

He placed a palm against her lower back and felt a slight shiver go through her. Unable to resist, he leaned down and pressed his lips against her neck. "I'd rather return to your apartment and test how strong your bed really is, but let's go see my mother."

Her eyes blazed with a passion that hadn't been there a moment ago. He loved how reactive she was to him.

The aroma of goat meat met them in the kitchen as his mother stirred a pot of soup. A rhythmic pounding came from outside the kitchen door as someone mashed casava and plantain into fufu.

"Good evening, Mama."

His mother looked up to find them watching her.

"Precious!" She ran and hugged her. "I prayed it was you. I'm so happy."

A lump formed in Osei's throat at his mother's reaction. The woman had raised him to be tolerant of everyone despite her husband's attitude. No matter what happened with his father, he knew he'd never lose his bond with her.

He turned and wiped the stubborn tears of relief that had escaped from his eyes. He stepped to the woman who had given him life and hugged her tight.

"Thank you, Mama," he croaked, choked with emotion.

She released him and touched his cheek. "You have made a wise choice. Your father will come around. You'll see."

The pounding in the back had stopped. Bismark and Serwaa came in carrying bowls of fufu and put them on the counter.

"Hi, Precious." His brother slapped him on the shoulder. "Hey, bro. You could've shown up a little earlier to pound. Serwaa almost took off my finger."

"If you'd ever learned to pound properly, I could've turned."

Bismark took a paper towel and wiped the sweat from Serwaa's neck. "And go through a workout just to eat? No, thank you."

Precious joined his family in the laughter, and Osei bowed his head in relief at their acceptance. Now to break down the one person who resisted.

***

The lunch with Osei's family had been better than Precious had expected. Having his siblings' and mother's support had made the meal bearable when his father continued on with the silent treatment. He had eventually thawed and joined in the joviality of the occasion, but he'd only spoken in Twi. Something he hadn't formerly done with her around.

She didn't know if he thought she couldn't speak the language of her father's people, but when she responded, he'd stopped to stare at her.

His eyes had narrowed. "Have you lived in Kumasi before? You speak Twi without an accent."

Not the time to get into her family history, she kept the response simple. "I used to visit Beposo a lot when I was younger."

Osei had changed the topic with an anecdote about one of his co-workers, easing the tension.

After dissecting everything that had happened during the meal as he drove her home, by the time they'd reached her apartment, she and Osei had been convinced his father was on his way to accepting their relationship.

She'd been so worried about the father and son that not a day had gone by without her asking Osei about how his father was treating him. She'd been relieved each time he mentioned his father hadn't changed in regards to how they communicated, but he tended to close off any conversation Osei brought up about her.

They'd revealed their couple status to her mother the next Saturday. She had been jubilant, and just as Precious had anticipated, questions about getting married had been asked rapid-fire. The absolute opposite of Mr Aboagye's response. When Precious told her what had happened, her mother had advised them about Mr Aboagye's behaviour with a proverb Osei had nodded sagely to, but Precious only pretended to understand.

"*A family is like a forest. When you are outside, it is dense. When you are inside, you see that each tree has its own position to occupy*," her mother had said in English with a single nod that made her look like what she'd said was the ultimate wisdom she could bestow.

When she'd asked Osei about the relevance of the proverb, he'd explained that his father's role in the family was the protector. And if they recognized it, they'd be able to help him understand that Precious was not a threat.

When her mother had gone to the kitchen, she'd given him the side eye because she hadn't gotten that interpretation from her mother's words. "You're making that up."

"Ask your mother."

"I can't. She'd throw back the proverb, *when the fool is told a proverb, its meaning has to be explained to him*. I understand that well enough to never want to hear it again."

His laughter had lasted longer than she'd ever heard, tickling her to join in.

And now, at work, she looked at her vibrating phone to see Mr Aboagye's name on the screen. Her sessions with him had ended over two weeks ago.

She bit the inside of her cheek as she hit the answer button. "Hello?"

"Good morning. This is Emmanuel Aboagye. Am I speaking with Precious Kpodo?" His voice sounded official and cold.

A tightness of dread formed in her belly. "Good morning, Mr Aboagye. This is Precious."

"Would you be able to meet me at the hospital tomorrow morning at eight o'clock? I have an appointment for a review, but they never start on time, and I was wondering if we could talk."

What could he have to discuss? Was he going to tell her not to date Osei anymore? She'd woken up in a cold sweat after having nightmares about that happening. Neither of them would make a scene in the middle of a crowded waiting room. Mr Aboagye was a private man who didn't like his business known to others. Perhaps he wanted to engage her services. For what, though? She'd done as much for him as she could.

"Yes, I can meet with you then," she responded, not able to dredge up the courage to ask him what the meeting pertained to.

"Good. Please don't tell anyone in my family, particularly Osei."

The hair at the back of her neck rose like a cat who had been threatened by a bear. Keeping as much respect in her voice as she could, she asked, "Why is that necessary, Mr Aboagye?"

"Because I requested it." The head master came out in full force. "Will you keep our meeting to yourself? If not, then never mind."

Curiosity about what he wanted to discuss piqued her interest. She could always tell Osei about it later. "I won't inform anyone."

"Good. I'll see you tomorrow."

It only took a second of realizing the phone had gone silent without a cordial goodbye to know she'd made a mistake.

Chapter Twenty-Three

As anticipated, every seat in the Outpatient Department was filled when Precious got there. It never ceased to amaze her how people could be late for almost every other appointment or activity, but when it came to seeing the doctor, they had no trouble being early.

She'd applied a heavier hand to her make-up to hide the bags she'd acquired from not sleeping last night. Her stomach was tied in knots with the fear of whatever Mr Aboagye had to say—she'd skipped breakfast, so now, she was feeling a little weak in addition.

Searching the room, she found the older version of Osei seated in a corner, his head bowed, reading a book. He'd told her during one of their sessions his voracity as a reader helped him climb the ladder of education to the position of head master he'd retired as.

Shoulders back and inwardly warning her heart it should slow down before it sent her to the Emergency Department, she went over to him. "Good morning, Mr Aboagye."

His gaze raised to hers slowly—no smile as he returned the greeting. "Is there somewhere we can speak privately?"

The unexpected request increased her anxiety. She had it on the tip of her tongue to decline before remembering she was no coward. He wouldn't try to hurt her, at least not physically. The consultants hadn't yet started seeing patients, so many rooms would be available for a few more minutes. "Will it take long?"

"No."

Precious pointed to the door closest to them. "We can use room four."

She watched as he got to his feet the way she'd taught him and used the cane for support when he stood. Internally, she clapped for how far he'd come. When she indicated he should lead, she assessed his gait. Strong and steady, with the expected glitch he'd most likely always possess. They'd made a wonderful team.

When they entered the room with a sheet-covered examination couch and a chair, he chose to remain standing and handed over the folder he'd been carrying.

"What's this?"

"Open it," he ordered.

A quick scan of the forms inside didn't shed any light on the contract of partnership she'd read. "I don't understand."

"It's paperwork establishing me as a silent partner in your rehabilitation centre so you can acquire a loan. With the number of properties I own, no bank would deny me a loan."

Had he truly accepted her as Osei's girlfriend and wanted to help? The character of the man wouldn't allow her to believe it. "But, why?"

His gaze held none of the friendliness she'd come to expect from him. "I'm willing to help you if you leave Osei. Forever."

Legs wobbly, she sank into the chair and had to readjust herself so she didn't slip off and land on the floor. "Pardon me?"

"There's no longer a need to be cunning. You heard me. I don't want you with my son. He has a promising future in front of him, and he doesn't need you dragging him down. Damn people infiltrating my home and stealing what's mine. That will never happen again," he mumbled. "I'm too aware of your ways now."

"Did I do something to offend you, Mr Aboagye? Or did something happen to make you hate my people?" Or at least the half he had no regard for.

A chill stole down her spine as his eyes looked through her and the room became deathly silent.

"They befriended me," he said after a minute. "My uncle had warned me not to trust them because they were Ewes. They only look after and cared for themselves, everyone else is dispensable to them. I didn't listen and snuck around to meet with them. Elenyam and Seli were my friends, and Dzifa said she loved me."

He reached up and touched the back of his head. "I had earned my uncle's trust enough for him to give the responsibility of driving his truck to town and purchasing the bags of chicken feed for the week. One day, Dzifa joined me. I should've known something was wrong when she seemed on edge. At one point, she told me to stop the vehicle because she felt ill. When I got out to join her on the side of the road, someone hit me on the back of the head, and I stumbled to my knees. I turned to find my *friends*," he snarled. "One holding a brick, and the other looking through the truck. I crawled towards the vehicle, and Elenyam hit me again. I landed flat on my face, only to hear Seli yell that he'd gotten the money."

Precious sat as still as the furniture, the air thick with the pressure of the story as she waited for its completion.

He sagged a little heavier on his cane. "I forced myself to roll onto my back. I was sure my life would end that day as through blurred vision, I saw Elenyam standing above me with the raised brick. Dzifa screamed out and rammed into Elenyam. I didn't understand the argument they'd had, but as I tried to get to my feet, someone kicked me in the ribs, and I curled into a ball gasping for breath. And then, I heard the truck drive away. At that moment, I knew it would've been better if Elenyam had killed me because my uncle would finish the job anyway."

The slow shake of his head didn't extract him from his reverie. "My uncle beat me mercilessly for it. It took me days to recover, and if it hadn't been for the pleading of my sisters and the truck being found in town the next day, he would have sent me back to Mpasaso. Away from the education I knew would get me the kind of life I'd always dreamed about. All because I hadn't listened to my uncle. Never would I trust an Ewe again."

He regained focus after a few seconds. As if realizing what he'd admitted, he flicked a hand towards the paper. "You're a good physiotherapist who has helped me tremendously. I believe you'll do well with your rehabilitation centre when you open it. The offer has two conditions. You must leave my son, and you can never tell anyone about this."

Despite why he was doing it, Mr Aboagye was giving her a chance at fulfilling her vision sooner rather than the years she'd resigned herself to. She'd been praying for such an opportunity.

Yet, it would mean giving up Osei, the man who held her heart.

But what if the feelings were one-sided? What if he didn't love her like Toyin had said, and he was with her for the good times they were having? Then she'd have given up this chance at advancing her career and helping so many in the process.

Her mouth parched, she struggled to speak. "What happens if I decline your offer?"

His gaze held her captive as he towered over her. "Then you'll know you have separated a man from his father and will have to live with that for the rest of your life. But, I'm sure you'll eventually disappoint Osei, and he'll figure out on his own who can be trusted. He'll come seeking forgiveness. And I'll give it because I love my son."

He tapped his cane on the floor twice. "It would be easier on all of us if you took my offer and prevented the inevitable from happening if you keep up this farce of a relationship. Despite working in a bank, Osei can't help you to acquire a loan. Unlike those papers in your hand."

Precious jumped to her feet, rage burning through her. How dare he? What did he know about her? He'd based a whole group of people on the three thieves who had deceived him years ago. "My father was an Ashanti. From Beposo."

He nodded slowly. "Osei informed me. This doesn't change the fact that you were raised by an Ewe woman and relate more with them than your Ashanti relatives. Do what is right for my son and let him go."

As if he'd been walking independently on a cane for years rather than a month, he made a dignified exit, leaving Precious in a state of stunned anger. Breathing as if she'd just completed a sprint, she became lightheaded and slowed her respirations until the examination cot no longer looked appealing to collapse onto.

She'd heard so many stories where the relationships between the two tribes hadn't worked out. The only one she'd cared about was her parents' own. Love hadn't been the issue. Their families and their cultural clinging of traditional lineage had. If she and Osei defied all the odds and worked out, what would happen to her children if anything happened to them?

Her mother wouldn't be around forever, and leaving her children with Lamisi was too much to ask. Would Osei's family care for children that came from the paternal line? He said they would, but with his father's backwards thinking and behaviour, she didn't know. Leaving her children in the same kind of peril she'd been deserted in would make her a wicked woman. She'd be selfish to only think of love and the pleasures it brought, and not of the future.

Was her and Osei's relationship doomed like Mr Aboagye had mentioned?

Lamisi's advice jumped into her head. *"Listen to your heart."*

Unfortunately, the thoughts were blocking whatever her heart was trying to reveal, creating even more confusion.

Chapter Twenty-Four

Back-to-back meetings had kept Osei from answering the message Precious had sent. He read her text as soon as he got into his office. *Can you stop by after work tonight? Any time would be fine.*

He responded with a quick yes and gave an estimated time to expect him. With all the work his boss had piled on his head, he hadn't intended to stop over, but he became excited at the prospect of seeing her after three days of not holding her. Speaking on the phone didn't eradicate how much he missed being with her live and in person. He sighed, wishing they could be together every day.

Marry her, then.

He sat up so fast, his rolling desk chair pushed back and slammed against the wall. Too soon to be thinking about marriage. He didn't know how she felt about him. And he hadn't told her how much he loved her. Yet, he couldn't have found a more spectacular woman.

They needed to get to know each other better before getting married. Didn't they?

The logical answers of *yes*, *definitely*, or *for sure* didn't pop into his head. Instead, a vision of his queen wearing a royal purple and gold Kente cloth that matched his as they danced together at their traditional wedding slid into his mind and stayed. It was replaced with him waiting for her at the altar as she glided down the aisle in a magnificent white dress.

His imagination came to a screeching halt as a knock sounded at his door. "Come in."

"Here is the file you asked for."

Osei accepted it. "Thank you, Martin."

Time to get his head out of the clouds and back to work. He'd take time later to consider what had prompted the image in the first place and what he'd do about it.

***

The moment she opened the door to her apartment, Precious jumped onto Osei, clinging to him as if she would blow away if she didn't. He struggled to gain his balance by grabbing the door frame before they both toppled to the ground. Stepping inside, he closed and locked the door before carrying her into the hall.

"Sweetheart, are you okay?"

The sniffle was a sure sign the answer lay in the negative, and his arms tightened around her once he'd settled her onto his lap.

"What's wrong?"

She raised her face. The tears streaming down her cheeks caused his own eyes to burn. He blinked and swallowed hard as he pulled out a handkerchief from his pocket and wiped her cheeks, vowing to punish whoever had caused her to cry.

When she opened her mouth to speak, the tears turned into sobs. Feeling helpless, he held her close and rocked her. He did a mental calculation about when she'd told him she had her period. It had only been three weeks ago. They'd spent time together then, and she hadn't been emotional. Not like his sister Dorcas could get. And definitely not like this.

He came up with all sorts of revenge tactics to apply to the source. The person would suffer twenty times what Precious was going through.

When the weeping abated, he kissed her temple. "I'm going to put you down and get you some water."

She nodded and slid onto the couch.

In the kitchen, he quickly acquired a sachet of water and poured it into a glass. He also wet a paper napkin.

"Here." He handed her the glass.

Precious took a few sips of the liquid and let out a stuttered sigh. "I'm sorry. I didn't mean for you to see me like that. As soon as I saw you..." Her eyes became glossy again as she took another drink.

Rather than press and risk having her cry, he gave her the wet paper towel and watched as she cleaned her face. And then, he waited.

She cleared her throat. "Thank you."

Was she joking? He'd done the bare minimum. "You're welcome."

"Yesterday, your father called and asked to meet with me at the hospital before his check-up. When we talked, he offered to let me use him as a silent partner to co-sign a loan if—" her lip quivered, and she took a drink of water. "If I let you go."

Wait...What? She couldn't have said what he'd heard.

"I don't understand."

"Neither did I at first." She took in a harsh breath before replaying the conversation she'd had with his father.

The paperwork in the folder she placed in his hand? All the proof he needed.

Fury, raw and fierce, held the potential of ripping open his chest. He stood and paced the length of the room. How could the man he'd looked up to and tried to emulate be so underhanded and manipulative? Controlling.

His father had been planning this for two weeks. Plying Osei into a false sense of security that he'd accepted his choice when the whole time, he'd been plotting to destroy his relationship with Precious. What had happened to his father had been traumatic and fear-inducing at the time, but he shouldn't hold it against a whole group of people and try to pass on the prejudice to his children. If it hadn't been for his mother's open mind and the people he'd befriended at school, Osei may have fallen into the trap of behaving in the same manner.

"Osei, you need to calm down."

After what his father had put Precious through, it would take a long time for that to happen. Pacing the room didn't expunge enough of his furious energy.

"At least now, you know where it stems from," she added. "It's not something ingrained from generations of thinking. Your father had a life-threatening experience and hasn't been able to forgive." She shrugged. "Maybe if he were guided in that direction, he'd change."

He focused on her and what she'd said. How had he received such a compassionate woman into his life? He didn't deserve her. And then, the realization that she'd chosen him over starting her own business hit. His angst momentarily forgotten, he sat next to her and cupped her face.

Looking into the depths of her eyes, his feelings for her bubbled up to the surface and couldn't be submerged. It may not be the most romantic moment, but the timing couldn't be any more perfect. "I love you, Precious."

He didn't need a reply, just to know she understood the depth of his feelings. He kissed her with the passion of his emotions, revelling in her taste, touch, sweet scent, and uninhibited responsiveness. He could be here with her like this until the heavenly chariots came swooping down and carried them away. Just as long as they were together, everything would be good.

Precious was the only one he'd ever thought about marrying. About spending the rest of his life with, and now, he knew his heart had been right all along.

She'd chosen him.

***

Why did Osei have to say the words she'd longed to hear? Because he'd waited until he was sure, it meant that much more. She wanted to accept his love and nurture it. To tell him how much she loved him in return, but she'd made a decision and was determined to abide by it. She wouldn't be cruel and utter the words that would give him hope.

Clinging to him one last time, she returned every caress and stroke of his tongue, but she couldn't let it get further than the kisses that would be branded into her memory forever. When he reached for the hem of her top, she held his hands still. With one last brush of his lips, she put some space between them, hoping it would be easier this way.

"Osei, we can't be together."

His head cocked to the side. "What?"

She'd never have guessed the hardest thing she'd do would be to let go of the man she loved after discovering he loved her in return. Where was the justice? Couldn't she at least have him when she'd already had so much loss?

Not if you want to live a happy life.

Staying with him would mean she'd always feel guilty about their relationship. The tears that had poured out of her when she'd opened the door to him had been for this moment. For the sake of healing his family.

"Your father loves all of his children, but you're his pride and joy. When he first started walking, using the parallel bars for support, I'd tell him to picture something or someone he wanted to reach on the other side. And he'd always make it, no matter how much it seemed he wanted to stop." Her heart was ripping into pieces. "Every time I asked him what he'd envisioned, he'd say you."

Osei's eyes widened.

"Yes. He wanted to make you proud of him. He loves you so much." A quick bite of her lower lip momentarily diverted the pain from her chest. "Your father holds you in high esteem. He bragged about all of you, but you came up the most. He'd talk about how far you've come in your career and how much more you'll accomplish. When he started talking about your woodwork, he'd beam and praise you as if he'd raised the most creative person who ever existed."

"Are we still talking about Emmanuel Aboagye? He's never said a word about my pieces other than commenting they were functional."

"To you. To me, he raved about your use of colour and texture. The way you were using reclaimed wood and saving the environment from having it burned. How he recommended to his friends that they go to the Blue Leaf Market and see your work. He possessed so much pride in his oldest child, it fuelled him to do his best to become independent faster." The air she exhaled came out uneven. "I can't get in the way of that. You still have so much more to learn about each other. Your father would break if you chose me over him, and I can't allow it to happen. Not after I spent so much time and energy helping to build him back up."

Osei snarled. "He can't control my life."

"I don't think that's his objective. He wants you to be happy. To not make the same mistakes he did." She held up a hand, still not believing she was defending the man who had attempted to bribe her into leaving Osei.

She'd been distracted and ineffective at work after the shock of the morning, so she'd requested to go home early. The time she'd spent lying on her couch contemplating the situation had brought her to a state of mercy and forgiveness.

"We both know we aren't a mistake." They were perfect together. She swallowed the threatening tears, wishing this wouldn't hurt so much. "But your father still regrets his past and takes it out on a whole group of people who don't deserve it. It's not right, but until he's willing to accept us together, I can't be with you. I refuse to be the one who gets in the way of a family."

"But he'll come around with time. We could still be together until he does."

"Your father is an arrogant man." She managed a weak smile. "You get it from him, but you've learned to be flexible. If you leave his home under these conditions, he'd take it personally. I fear your relationship would be fractured forever."

"It already is."

She placed a hand on his knee. "Don't say that. He's your father. I'd give anything to have my parents back. Anything."

He leaned forward until their foreheads touched. "We can still be together while my father is working out his issues."

If only they could. She would've presented that as her first and only option.

"We'd be sneaking around. Not how I want to live." *With the man I'm irrevocably in love with.*

"This doesn't make sense. How will my being without you help me get along with my father? I'll get angry every time I look at him because he's the cause of my misery. No. There's another way. There has to be." He got to his feet. "Let's think about this and come up with a smarter solution."

Osei was in as much denial as she still was. If he gave her one good reason to go against what she knew without a doubt was the correct thing to do, she'd leap into his arms and hold on for eternity. If his proclamation of love hadn't done it, then nothing he could say would make her ever believe breaking apart his family would turn out well. So, she kept her mouth shut and her tears banked.

"Wait." She went back to the coffee table and picked up the folder. "You can keep this."

He looked at the item as if it were a puff adder snake on the verge of striking. After a few seconds, he took it.

She reminded herself she was doing the right thing. If they were meant to be, then they would have been, without all of this family drama.

At the door, he leaned over and pressed his lips against hers in a lingering kiss. She memorized every sensation of being with him this last time.

When he pulled away, she didn't tell him to call her when he got home. And he didn't say he would. That's how she knew it was over.

Chapter Twenty-Five

"When are you returning to work?" his mother asked as she piled a crate of malt drinks onto another one.

Osei had been sitting at her shop for the past four days after calling in sick to work. Not a single person at his workplace had contacted him to see how he was doing, which added to the ire already brewing inside of him.

"You're always telling me to take some time off. Now that I have, you want to send me back?" He wished he could've said it in a joking manner, but his mother had meant every word.

"I'm always happy to have you around, but you've been brooding the whole time."

He couldn't argue with her there.

"What's wrong, Osei? It would make you feel better if you talked about it. Your scowl is scaring away my customers."

The one person he wanted to communicate with had blocked him. Precious hadn't responded to his calls or texts. When he'd stopped by her apartment, she hadn't answered the doorbell each day he'd tried. Yesterday evening, he'd gone to see Aunty Selorm. She'd only shaken her head and said in a tone filled with authority that he should give Precious time. And of course, she'd left him with a proverb, for the first time speaking to him in Twi. *"Woforo dua pa a na yepia wo."*

His mind so muddled with misery, he either hadn't wanted to understand the proverb or just couldn't. *It is when you climb a good tree that we push you.* Or maybe Precious was right and proverbs made no sense except to the one who spoke it.

"Precious broke up with me," he said to his mother.

She stopped stocking the sachets of liquor and sat in the plastic chair next to him. "What happened?"

After the completion of the story about his father's scheming ways, Theodora Aboagye placed a hand against her chest and sighed. "I knew Precious was a good person, but very few would give up so much to preserve someone else's family."

He wished she'd been selfish and thought more about their relationship than the one he had with his father. "Did you hear what I said about Dada offering to pay her off with the support of a loan and why he hates a whole group of people?"

"Yes. I heard. Your father is a complicated man. I knew about his past experience, but not what he'd been planning to do with Precious."

He was relieved she wasn't involved in the scheme. He dipped his head and looked at his mother as if he were a lie detector. "Would you have tried to stop him if you had known?"

"Of course I would have. What he did was wrong. And yet, I'm glad Precious passed whatever test he put her through."

His ears smarted. "Test?"

"You know your father always has some kind of a master plan behind everything he does. Not even suffering a stroke would rob him of that."

Osei scraped a hand down his face. "I don't understand."

"Well, then, speak to your father." She got to her feet when a customer came. "You've been avoiding him."

When he went to speak, she cut him a look that told him to keep whatever he was going to say contained. The gears in his head created smoke from how fast they were turning. And he still couldn't make sense of it.

The customers kept coming. He'd be better off swallowing his pride and going to talk to his father than to wait for his mother's input. She'd only give him the same advice. He served some customers and waited until the shop assistant had returned from lunch.

"I'm going home."

"Already?"

The sarcasm blared at him, and he grinned. "I'll see you back at the house."

"Be patient with your father, Osei. Whether you agree with him or not, everything he does is in the best interest of his family."

The man had made his life a living hell, and he was supposed to consider him to be benevolent? The walk home would do him good to help settle his fluctuating rage. When he wasn't livid, misery clutched at him.

As he stepped onto the compound, for a split second, he thought of ignoring his mother's advice and going to pack his things to move into a hotel until he could find his own place. A vision of Precious' face stopped him. If he didn't work things out with his father, then they'd never be together.

Unlocking the door, he stepped into the home his parents had built from the ground up. Expecting his father to be in his chair in the hall, Osei was thrown when he walked past the kitchen and saw him sitting on a chair in front of the stove with the scent of stew and boiling rice filling the air.

"Are you hungry, Osei? I made Kontomire stew. Don't tell your mother, but I added a little more palm oil than I should have. I figured this one time wouldn't hurt."

His father speaking to him as if he hadn't just ruined his life threw him even further into a whirl of confusion. Maybe he didn't know. Osei hadn't spoken to him out of fear he'd cross a line of disrespect. Despite his actions, his father would always be the one who'd taken care of him and taught him how to be a man.

"No, thank you. Mama and I ate red-red at the shop." The sweet fried plantain and bean stew they'd purchased didn't compare to anything that came from their home, but it had been filling.

His father got to his feet and stirred the stew.

What a difference a few months of therapy had made. All thanks to Precious.

Despite wanting to get everything out in the open, Osei wouldn't disturb his father's meal with such a heavy conversation. "Do you need any help?"

"As long as I take my time, I'm fine."

Osei waved in the direction of the bedrooms. "I'm going to my room. I'll be back out when you're done."

His father caught his eye before he could leave. The man looked tired. "You could come sit with me and talk. We haven't done that for a few days."

The unexpected offer shifted his ire to a simmer, and he nodded. "I'll meet you in the dining room."

Osei went to his room and clenched his jaw as he picked up the folder Precious had handed him. He made it to the table before his father and slid the paperwork on the seat next to him.

The tapping of the cane against the tiled floor with the slight shuffle of slippered feet and a grunt almost had him jumping up to help his father. The older man would resent it when he could do it himself. How could his father not see how invasive he'd been in his life when he insisted on such fierce independence in his?

His father settled into his seat, bowed his head, and said a short prayer out loud before looking up at Osei and grinning. "You're invited."

"Thank you," he declined with a smile of his own at the tradition of offering whoever was in their company food. Done out of politeness, mostly, but if the individual needed to eat, the sharing of the food would be genuine.

His father ate a few forkfuls. "Your mother tells me you've been with her at the shop. Is everything okay at work?"

It looked like they were going to have polite conversation until he could get to what was gutting him. "I decided to take a few days off."

"That's not like you. Are you well?"

Not wanting to ruin his father's meal with something as trivial as the truth, he nodded. "Yes. I needed some time off. How are you feeling?"

His father flexed his left hand. "I'm strong, but I know I could have more power in this arm." As he ate, he spoke about how he would be doing what they called occupational therapy at the hospital and the difference between it and the physiotherapy Precious had put him through. "Precious recommended it before she left."

Osei found it strange how his father had mentioned her name with absolutely no animosity. And yet, he'd treated her as if she were worth nothing. When his father had cleared his plate, Osei took the folder and placed it on the table.

"Precious told me about the deal you tried to make with her." He could barely recognize the harshness of his own voice.

His father looked down at the evidence. "I see."

"What were you thinking, Dada? Why did you drive her away?"

Expressionless, his gaze remained on the folder as he tapped it. "It was for your own good."

"To force her out of my life? You've never kept it a secret you don't like the Ewes, but to do this is wretched."

"It's not that I don't like them. I don't trust them. The experience I had when I was younger nearly cost me my life and the future I had envisioned. It's kept me bitter. Despite my occasional comments, I have never shown partiality against any of my students."

No complaint had ever been made against his father as a teacher or head master that he'd ever heard of.

"I regret the man I've portrayed to you over the years," his father continued. "My behaviour was wrong and should never have been tolerated. Not in word or deed. As a family, you have been trying to tell me this for years, but I refused to listen. My heart was hardened by an experience I should have released long ago."

The conversation had derailed in a direction Osei no longer had control over, so he remained quiet.

"Have you noticed I haven't spoken badly about them in the past month?"

Osei went through his memory. "I hadn't noticed."

"Well, I haven't, and it's been intentional. Old habits die hard, so it took me a while to adjust my thinking about Ewes. Something I should've done a long time ago." He dipped his chin as if disappointed in himself. "On the second day of my rehabilitation with Precious, I noticed you two liked each other."

He hadn't even known himself at that point. Yes, he'd been attracted to her, but that was all. *Liar.*

His father shook his head and frowned. "Not in my wildest imaginings did I ever think any of my children would end up with anyone who wasn't Akan, never mind an Ewe."

"Ghana is mixed up now. All the tribes encounter each other and interact. It was inevitable."

His father nodded. "I understood it on a logical level, but I was still angry. I almost told Precious it would be her last day working with me."

"Why didn't you?"

"Because that day, I took my first steps. Precious was patient and encouraging. I couldn't let her go and risk not getting a better therapist because of my own prejudices. When it came to you and a potential association with her, I had a choice to make. Either I let go of the past and move forward, or like so many of my friends, I try to control who you attempt to be with and lose our relationship."

Osei jumped to his feet so he towered over his father. "You chose to try to control me. It won't work."

He was about to storm off when his father's voice penetrated past his wrath.

"No, son. I chose to show you the truth."

CHAPTER TWENTY-SIX

Precious never thought she'd be back at the Aboagye residence, but not even twenty minutes had passed since Mrs Aboagye had called and asked her to come help with an urgent matter with her husband. With her work shift almost done and fear galvanizing her, she'd rushed through the paperwork she'd been completing and had hurried right over.

Her mother would say her heart was too soft for her own good. Anyone else would've told Osei's mother to call someone else. Not her, though. Always a sucker to ease someone else's pain, here she was.

The door remained unanswered, so she hit the doorbell again.

A moment later, the pathway gate swung open, and she stumbled back with a gasp. She couldn't tear her gaze away from the tall, richly dark-skinned man who had caused the same reaction the first day she'd met him. She'd moved back in with her mother to avoid him, and now, the fantasy and nightmare of seeing him again materialized.

"What are you doing here?" she asked.

He was supposed to be at work. He was always at work. For the past four days, she'd gone onto the Allegiant Bank compound to search for his car hoping to catch a glimpse of him to ease her torment. She would've slunk away if he'd been around, but his car had never shown up.

When her mother had told her he'd stopped by the other day, she'd been relieved. Her mind knew that anything to do with him was none of her business, but her heart couldn't stop wondering and caring about him. It hurt that love couldn't be shut off like faucet.

"I took a few days off," Osei answered.

"Oh."

"Look, Precious—"

"Your mother called and asked me to come over." She couldn't deal with whatever he was about to say. Even hearing his voice scraped against the rawness of her emotions. "Is everything okay?"

His brows rose, but he stood speechless.

"Both of you, please come in," Mr Aboagye said from the veranda.

Seeing that everything was okay and she wasn't needed, she pivoted and took a step towards the gate.

"Precious," the older man called out. "Please, let me explain."

She sighed. If Mr Aboagye had gone to the lengths of involving his wife in getting her there, then it must be important. Osei followed her into his home.

Once they'd settled in their seats in the hall, Osei asked, "Would you like some water?"

"No, thank you." What she wanted was to cuddle up next to him and start over as if they'd never had to separate. To hear him once again say he loved her and respond with the truth. It would never happen.

Mr Aboagye pointed to the infamous folder of betrayal. "You told my son everything."

"Yes."

He narrowed his eyes. "Why?"

Whatever curve she'd had in her back left as she straightened and pushed her chest and chin out. "He needed to know what you'd done and why."

"And you broke things off with him. Why?"

The answer that wasn't any of his business renewed the anger she'd tried desperately over the past few days to control. "That's between Osei and me."

A smile appeared on Mr Aboagye's face. "Can you please oblige me with an answer? Osei hasn't mentioned why. I can make presumptions, but I'd rather deal with the facts from you."

She stole a glance at Osei to find him with his head bowed, looking at his folded hands. What was going on? It was too late for them, but maybe the confession would help heal the father-son bond. "I didn't want to stand in the way of your relationship."

Mr Aboagye tapped the folder against his lap. "But you could've broken it off with him without telling him about my offer. By informing him, you gave up both your goal of getting a loan and my son. I thought I knew you to be a smart woman, but it doesn't sound like an intelligent move to me."

"Dada, I won't have you insulting Precious. What is this all about?"

Touched by his defence, she reached over and place a hand against his shoulder for the briefest of moments.

The electric shock reminded her the physical attraction they'd shared was still alive.

"It's all right. I'll answer. Accepting the arrangement was never part of my plan. My dream is there, waiting for me to fulfil it. I don't need to do it right now when I know there'll be a time when I'm in the right position to make it work out. I told Osei so he'd understand what lengths you'd go to protect him from what you thought was a threat."

She broke eye contact by looking down and blinked away the burn behind her eyes. There would be no tears shed during this conversation. "I understand how important it is to have family, and I couldn't be the one to take his away from him. So, I ended the relationship."

Other than the hum of the refrigerator in the kitchen, silence reigned.

"I wish my wife could have been here, but it's difficult to get her away from the shop once she opens it. Sometimes, I think she loves that place more than her own home." Mr Aboagye was the only one who laughed. And then, he sobered. "Your decision was commendable." He looked at his son. "I haven't seen you as happy as you've been in the past few months since before you started working at Allegiant Bank. I didn't realize how much the work drained you until recently. Precious is good for you. She helps you to remember the lighter aspects of life, and I appreciate that."

Precious and Osei glanced at each other for a quick moment. If he was thinking the same as her, then confusion resembled a wild flurry of cotton floss in his head, too.

"Was this some kind of absurd test?"

The sharpness in Osei's voice caused Mr Aboagye's mouth to purse in warning.

He was still an elder who they had both been taught to respect.

"It was a strategic move to understand Precious' true motives when it came to you."

Didn't he realize how he'd hurt his son? If she had been a different type of person, she would've taken the offer and left Osei. She'd left him anyway, not for selfish reasons, but because she loved him too much to see him lose what he would regret having given up for her.

"I needed to know Precious was different," Mr Aboagye said to his son. "And now that she's proven it, you may proceed with the relationship."

Osei's expression was unreadable from the side angle she viewed him from, but his features hadn't moved.

"Are you saying you've gotten over your issues with her being an Ewe?" His voice sounded calm, but his tightened shoulders and hands in balled fists stated otherwise.

"I have accepted that you have chosen to be with Precious, and I approve."

Osei shook his head. "You should have trusted me."

Standing, he looked down at Precious. "Let's go."

It took a moment to understand what had just happened. When she realized she could finally be with Osei with his father's blessing, she was relieved, excited, and scared she'd already lost him. She got to her feet and looked at Mr Aboagye. The crestfallen look on his face almost made her feel sorry for him.

Almost. He couldn't play with people's emotions and not pay the consequences. "Have a good evening, Mr Aboagye."

"Thank you, Precious." His voice sounded defeated as his gaze trailed his son's form as he left the home he'd tried to make safe for his family.

She met Osei outside. What would happen between them now? Was he also upset with her for breaking up with him? Her decision had been the one her gut had decided on, and she didn't regret it despite having missed him so much, she'd changed her mind a thousand times in the few days they'd been apart.

He led her to his workspace and undid the lock. The convoluted thoughts stopped when he opened the door and she saw how many new items filled the area. Nervous, she allowed herself to be distracted by the gorgeous pieces he'd created, admiring his handiwork. The several mirrors hanging against the walls framed in a variety of highly polished reclaimed wood of different shapes drew her to them. She caressed the largest one as she looked into the mirror to find Osei observing her.

Her smile was tentative as she caught his eye in the reflection. "You've been busy."

"The result of taking time off from work and not being able to sleep. Creating helps me to deal with my stress."

She glided her fingers against a coffee table she wanted to claim as her own. "Lucky customers."

"Thank you."

As if he understood she needed the time to compose herself, he remained still as she shuffled through the multitudes of new coasters and accented cutting boards. When her heart had settled into a steady rhythm, she finally turned to face him.

***

Osei clasped his trembling hands behind his back. Being in the same space with Precious again lingered on the cusp of too much to bear. When she finally pivoted, he gave in to longing and cleared the few feet between them.

Realizing he had no right to touch her, he stopped. "I've missed you."

Her eyes held his.

"Me, too." Her voice came out breathy. "Your father—"

"Did what he thought was right. I understand, but I'm not ready to let him know yet. I figure a few hours of thinking I'm unforgivably upset will give him pause before he interferes in his children's lives again."

Precious placed a hand against her chest and released a heavy breath. "I'm glad. To be honest, it sounds like something my mother would do. She's always the one to test people."

He grunted. "It wasn't right."

"Whenever she does it, she justifies it with one of her annoying proverbs. *It is when you climb a good tree that we push you.*"

He frowned as he recalled the saying being thrown at him. "I didn't understand when she said it. What does it mean?"

Arched brows rose. "The great proverb decipherer doesn't know?"

He grinned at her teasing tone, the tightness in his chest loosening. "Not this one."

"She explained it to me without harassment when I asked. The elders in a society can only support a good cause and not a bad one. In order to gain their support, a person needs to do good things they can support."

His mind turned the proverb and its interpretation over and around. "My father's test was for you, and she approved of it."

"Yes. Osei." Her throat bobbed with a hard swallow. "I'm sorry for causing you pain. I wanted everything to be okay between you and your father."

He sucked in a deep breath taking in the dominant scent of his beloved wood. "I understand, and I appreciate you cared so much about me you would give us up, but Precious…"

"Yes."

"I don't want to lose you again. I can't."

She placed a soothing hand against his cheek. "If you behave, you won't. I love you, Osei."

The warmth of her touch soothed the ache he'd experienced, and he vowed to do everything in his power to make her happy. "I love you, too. I can't promise to be perfect, but I vow to do the best I can to do right by you. But can we discuss things before you make a unilateral decision again?"

"Sounds fair. As long as I can misbehave all I want," she said with a mischievous sparkle in her eyes.

He wiggled his brows. "You have carte blanche when it comes to sex, but otherwise, the same rules you apply to me apply to you."

She closed the small space separating them and pressed her soft body against his. "Accepted. Now kiss me."

With his crafts to witness, the touch of their lips sealed their promise of love.

Epilogue

Precious handed out a card advertising Infinity Furniture and Handiwork. Osei's business had taken off in the past year. A week after their one and only break-up, he had discussed with her the possibility of him quitting his job at Allegiant Bank. She had been completely on board with a decision she knew would make him happy and decrease his stress levels. Taking a pay cut to work at a job as a human resource officer at a private hospital in Accra gave him more time to create bespoke items for people who requested them. The supplemental income from his crafts more than made up for the money he'd lost when he'd changed jobs.

Four months ago, at a wedding Osei had insisted on being an instrumental part of planning, she had reclaimed her Ashanti heritage and become an Aboagye. The traditional wedding with close family and friends had been picture-perfect with them wearing matching purple and gold Kente Osei said he'd envisioned them in within a few months of them meeting. She'd fallen in love with the cloth the instant he'd revealed it to her. From that moment on, she'd decided to leave the wedding planning to his creative eye, with her insisting on choosing the wedding cake.

If Ghana had a wedding television show displaying the most gorgeous weddings in the country, theirs would have made the list. Lamisi as her matron-of-honour was gorgeous. Osei's sisters as her bridesmaids had been on the verge of making her look dowdy. She feared Ghanaians weren't progressive enough for a bride's man, so at her request, Osei had allowed Toyin to be one of his groomsmen.

Before her mother walked her down the aisle, Precious had expected a proverb to come from her mouth. Instead, the woman had brought tears to her eyes when she'd said in Ewe, "Raising you has been one of the greatest pleasures of my life. You are the daughter of my heart, and every day, I thank God for the blessing of being your mother. I'm proud of the woman you have become and take great honour in helping you to become her. No one will ever love you more than I do, but I am sure Osei will certainly try."

And he had, beyond her wildest fantasies. He was everything she'd ever hoped for in a partner, and they kept growing closer. Every day was an adventure with him. Some better than others, but she had no regrets about their ongoing journey together.

And after the debacle his father had created in their relationship, as a wedding gift, Mr Aboagye had ended up making good on his offer to help her get a loan. She'd respectfully declined, fully understanding that business and family don't mix. There was no doubt she'd open her rehabilitation centre one day. Until then, life would be lived to the absolute fullest with Osei.

Thank you for reading Love and Handicrafts by Nana Prah. If you enjoyed this story, please leave a review on the site of purchase.

Connect with Nana: https://www.nanaprah.com/

OTHER BOOKS BY NANA PRAH
Healing His Medic
Be My Valentine Anthology Volume 1

ROYAL HOUSE OF SAENE SERIES
His Defiant Princess
The Resolute Prince

ARTISTS OF GHANA SERIES
Love and Hiplife
Love and Handicrafts

OTHER BOOKS BY LOVE AFRICA PRESS

Dating Mr Famous by Glory Abah
Rough Diamond by Kiru Taye
Falling for Her Bad Boy Boss by Zee Monodee
Let The Hear Beat by Jomi Oyel

CONNECT WITH US
Facebook.com/LoveAfricaPress
Twitter.com/LoveAfricaPress
Instagram.com/LoveAfricaPress

SIGN UP TO OUR NEWSLETTER
https://www.loveafricapress.com/newsletter

www.ingramcontent.com/pod-product-compliance
Lightning Source LLC
Chambersburg PA
CBHW030258100526
44590CB00012B/442